BEOWULF IN IRAQ

Lessons from an Ancient Warrior for the Modern Age

T.M. Johnson, M.D.

BEOWULF IN IRAQ

Lessons from an Ancient Warrior
for the Modern Age

BEOWULF IN IRAQ

Cover design by www.jeroentenberge.com

Grateful acknowledgement is made to Professor Dennis Hensely, Paul and Gisele Johnson, and Dr. J. Tavee for assistance and encouragement in writing this book.

TABLE OF CONTENTS

INTRODUCTION

Beowulf is an ancient poem about a mighty warrior written sometime around the tenth century AD. In the poem Beowulf fights not just men, but also a monster named Grendel, then Grendel's vengeful mother; finally, he fights and is killed by a dragon. The poem is written in Old English, a language that is very different from modern English. The names and places in the poem are unfamiliar to most of us today. *Beowulf* is now read mainly by high school and college students to satisfy a requirement for graduation. It is usually forgotten about once the course is over. The people who go on to study *Beowulf* further are typically English teachers, historians, sociologists, anthropologists, and other academics.

The poem was not written for professors and scholars living in ivory towers. It was written by and for the people of medieval England and northern Europe. They lived in a violent, harsh world where starvation, pestilence, and warfare were endemic. *Beowulf* is not just a fairy tale about a hero who lived a long time ago and fought scary monsters. It is about the tremendous physical and psychological demands placed on warriors who defend their people from enemy attack. It is about how an individual's pursuit of personal success and fame impacts, for good or ill, the community in which he or she lives. A central theme of the poem is that a society needs warriors who value honor, reputation, and adhere to the code of *comitatus,* the willingness to sacrifice self for the good of the group, in order to protect that society and allow it to survive. This is as true now as it was when the poem was first written. The goal of this book is to demonstrate that *Beowulf* is not just a work of literature from the distant past. It is also a guide for what is needed to ensure that America's warriors develop not just the fighting skills, but also the sense of honor and *comitatus* they need to defend our country from the monsters of our own time.

CHAPTER 1
The Poem

Nobody knows the exact origins of *Beowulf.* The Anglo-Saxons who composed it sometime around 1000 AD migrated from Scandinavia to England years before the poem was ever written down. It may have always been one long poem; could have started out as several smaller stories and poems that were combined into one epic over time by one or more authors. It is likely several versions of the poem existed in oral form for some time prior to its being put into written form. The poem deals with pre-Christian topics but was committed to writing by Christians. It contains elements of both pagan and Christian worldviews. There have been many translations over the years from Old English into modern English. This book relies exclusively on *Beowulf: A New Verse Translation,* by Seamus Heaney. [i]

The first character introduced in the poem is Shield Sheafson. It is never explained where he came from; simply that he began life as a foundling and grew to become a man of "courage and greatness." He leads a band of warriors and becomes known as:

> ...wrecker of mead benches, rampaging among foes. This terror of hall-troops had come far...In the end each clan on the outlying coasts beyond

the whale road [sea] had to yield to him and begin
to pay tribute.

Shield Sheafson is not just a ferocious fighter. He is
also the creator of a new kingdom. When he dies, he
leaves behind him a vigorous society strong enough to ex-
tract tribute from other tribes and rich enough to provide
him with a magnificent funeral. In the words of the poet,
"That was one good king." [ii]
Shield Sheafson has a son named Beow. As a young
prince, Beow knows it is important to "give freely while
his father lives so that afterwards in age when fighting
starts steadfast companions will stand by him and hold
the line." [iii] Beow is generous with gifts to his father's war-
fighters when he is a young man and his father is alive, in
order to ensure that he has their allegiance after his father
is gone. When Shield Sheafson dies, it falls to Beow to
defend the kingdom his father has built. The poem tells us
Beow "[keeps] the forts." This line makes it clear that the
Sheafson dynasty has gone from rampaging through rival
tribes' mead halls to building and maintaining fortifications to protect the lands they have conquered.
Beow has several children, and one of them, Halfdane,
succeeds him to become king. Halfdane is a "fighter king"
[iv] who has four children. One of his sons, Hrothgar, in-
herits the kingdom when Halfdane dies. The fortunes of
war favor Hrothgar, and "friends and kinsmen [flock] to
his ranks." He expands upon his forefather's accomplish-
ments and accumulates even more wealth and power. In
Hrothgar's domain there is "paved track,"[v] or roads, re-
vealing the increasingly sophisticated infrastructure in the
kingdom.

The lands ruled by the Sheafson dynasty continue to prosper. Hrothgar eventually decides to build a magnificent hall that displays the wealth, power, and increasing refinement and sophistication of his court. It is where his throne is to be located, and is the center of the new nation he and his fellow "Spear Danes" have created in a world filled with savage, warring tribesmen:

> It stood there, finished and ready, in full view, the hall of halls. Heorot was the name he had settled on it… The hall towered, its gables wide and high and awaiting… meant to be a wonder of the world forever…[vi]

It is not just a pile of timber, nor is it just another fort built for refuge or a base for launching raids against other tribes. It is a place of government, where Hrothgar's word "[becomes] rule of law." It is a center for feasting and celebration, a meeting place for people to exchange stories and sing songs. It symbolizes the success of the civil society Shield Sheafson and his descendants have built over generations.

The construction of Heorot and the growth of Hrothgar's kingdom do not go unnoticed. The poem tells us about a creature named Grendel. He is of the "clan of Cain" and hates Hrothgar and his Spear Danes and their hall. The poem provides a good description of what Grendel looks like. He is "warped in the shape of a man… [but] bigger than any man." [vii] There is no evidence that Grendel and his clan have the technological ability or social cohesion to build a magnificent hall like Heorot. In fact, Grendel lives in a cave with his mother. It is a home

that seems wet, cold, lonely, and depressing in comparison to Heorot.

Grendel and his mother roam the inaccessible moors
and rough terrain at the margins of Hrothgar's kingdom.
Grendel does not speak a single word in the poem, and
it is not clear if he has the power of speech. It is never
explained how he got the name Grendel. He is stronger
than any Dane. He has no weapons other than his natural strength and cunning. His hide is impervious to the
Danish weapons. Grendel bears a "hard grudge" against
Hrothgar and begins attacking the hall at night, devour-
ing any warrior he can lay his hands on and then disap-
pearing back into the darkness. Soon the beautiful hall
is an empty shell the Danes avoid after dark, no longer a
symbol of Hrothgar's power but instead one of his impo-
tence against Grendel's attacks.

These attacks go on for twelve long years. These are
"hard times…heartbreaking" for Hrothgar;[viii] he is a king,
able to lead his people to victory in war against other
tribes, but he is powerless against Grendel. Word spreads
throughout the region of his desperate plight. Over the
years many brave warriors come to spend the night in the
hall and fight Grendel. They are all dead by morning. The
Danes become desperate. They make sacrifices at pagan
shrines to the Old Norse gods, begging for some sort of
intervention, but get no response. The poem states:

That troubled time continued, woe that never stopped,
steady affliction for Halfdane's son, too hard an ordeal.
There was panic after dark, people endured raids in the
night, riven by the terror…[ix]

A warrior named Beowulf of the Geat tribe, from some-
where in southern Sweden, hears of Hrothgar's plight. He

is the nephew of Hygelac, king of the Geats. He has a reputation for strength but is not a particularly wealthy or prominent person in Geat society. The poem tells us that in his younger days Hrothgar helped a member of Beowulf's extended family, and Beowulf's entire family therefore has an obligation to help Hrothgar in order to repay this debt. Beowulf travels to Hrothgar's kingdom to battle Grendel. He knows that if he succeeds, he will have repaid his family's obligation to Hrothgar. He will also win fame and fortune by killing this notorious monster.

> He ordered a boat that would ply the waves. He announced his plan: to sail the swan's road and search out that king [Hrothgar], the famous prince who needed defenders. Nobody tried to keep him from going. No elder denied him… he moved about like the leader he was, enlisting men, the best he could find; with fourteen others the warrior boarded the boat as captain… Over the waves, with the wind behind her…she flew like a bird…at the due hour, those seafarers sighted land. It was the end of their voyage.[x]

When he arrives in Hrothgar's kingdom he first meets one of the Hrothgar's men assigned to guard the coast. The watchman is immediately impressed by the physical size, the quality of weaponry, and the noble bearing of Beowulf and his men. He escorts Beowulf and his fellow Geats to Heorot Hall, where Hrothgar holds court during the day but flees at night out of fear of the marauding Grendel.

King Hrothgar has heard of Beowulf even before he arrives at Heorot through stories told to him by sailors. The old king knows who Beowulf is related to and that he has come both to fulfill a social obligation and to win fame and honor for himself. He also knows through his connections with sailors and other sources of information that Beowulf is an amazingly strong man. He is embarrassed that he and his fellow Spear Danes cannot take care of their "Grendel problem," but he is desperate and accepts Beowulf's offer to help rid him of this monster.

When Beowulf arrives at the court he tells Hrothgar he has come to fight and kill or be killed by Grendel in hand-to-hand combat. Not everyone at Heorot appreciates Beowulf's offer to rid the hall of Grendel. One member of the court, Unferth, questions Beowulf's integrity and ability to fight a monster that has defeated so many other warriors. He does this by asking if Beowulf is the man of the same name who several years ago challenged an individual named Breca to a swimming contest on the open sea, a bet that placed the lives of both men at risk over what Unferth insinuates was a frivolous swimming race; and that in the end, Breca was the better swimmer. The implication is that if Beowulf cannot even win a swimming contest, the he does not stand a chance against Grendel. Beowulf explains that he and Breca were childhood friends who always challenged each other in friendly competitions to encourage themselves to excel at physical tests and challenges such as swimming. He says the truth of the matter is that he is a much stronger swimmer than Breca, but in the course of the swimming match the weather turned foul, and he was attacked by sea monsters:

The perishing cold, night falling and the winds from the north drove us apart. The deep boiled up and its wallowing sent the sea brutes wild. My armour helped me to hold art: my hard ringed chain-mail, hand-forged and linked, a fine, close-fitting, filigree of gold, kept me safe when some ocean creature pulled me to the bottom. Pinioned fast and swathed in its grip, I was granted one final chance: my sword plunged and the ordeal was over. Through my own hands, the fury of the battle had finished off the sea-beast. Time and again, foul things attacked me, lurking and stalking, but I lashed out, gave as good as I got with my sword. My flesh was not for feasting on, there would be no monsters gnawing and gloating over their banquet at the bottom of the sea. Instead, in the morning, mangled and sleeping the sleep of the sword, they slopped and floated like the ocean's leavings. From now on sailors would be safe…my sword had killed nine sea-monsters….[xi]

Beowulf managed to survive the stormy seas and the attack by monsters, but in so doing he became exhausted to the point of nearly drowning, until he finally washed ashore on the coast of Finland. Beowulf goes on to point out that if Unferth

were truly…keen and courageous…Grendel would have never gotten away with such un-checked atrocity, attacks on your king, havoc in Heorot and horrors everywhere.

Beowulf goes on to mention that Unferth, for all his "cleverness and quick tongue…will suffer damnation in the depths of Hell"[xii] for having murdered one of his kinsmen in a feud. Unferth is silent, and the members of Hrothgar's court are satisfied with Beowulf's response.

After the introductions have been completed, the Danes and Geats sit down to a feast together. The Geats hear from the Danes firsthand about Grendel's strength and savagery. Hrothgar laments the difficult situation he and his fellow Danes are in. They have suffered not only death and destruction but also humiliation because they cannot defeat the monster. Hrothgar tells of their misfortune:

> …time and time again, when the goblets passed and seasoned fighters got flushed with beer, they would pledge themselves to protect Heorot and wait for Grendel with whetted swords. But when dawn broke and day crept in over each empty, blood-spattered bench, the floor of the mead hall where they had feasted would be slick with slaughter. And so they died, faithful retainers, and my following dwindled. [xiii]

Hrothgar's men lost their lives in defense of their king and hall, fulfilling their duties of service to their king Hrothgar. In contrast, Hrothgar cannot perform his duty as a king and devise a strategy to lead his men to victory over Grendel. If this continues long enough, it could mean the end of his kingdom and complete victory for Grendel.

As darkness approaches, the Danes leave the hall, but the Geats remain and await an attack from Grendel:

> None of them expected he would ever see his homeland or get back to his native place and the people who reared him. They knew too well the way it was before, how often the Danes had fallen prey to death in the mead hall.[xiv]

In spite of this, none of them sneaks out of the hall or deserts Beowulf. In the dark of the night, Grendel arrives. The monster grabs and devours one of Beowulf's companions. Beowulf is awake, but he remains perfectly still:

> Mighty and canny... keenly watching for the first move the monster would make. Nor did the creature keep him waiting... His talon was raised to attack Beowulf where he lay on the bed; he was bearing in with open claw when the alert hero's comeback and armlock forestalled him utterly. The captain of evil discovered himself in a handgrip harder than anything he had ever encountered in any man on the face of the earth.[xv]

In the past Grendel had used the cover of darkness as part of his strategy to surprise his human enemies while they slept, but Beowulf is able to achieve tactical surprise because the time and place of Grendel's attacks are predictable. Beowulf is able to get such a grip on Grendel that the creature cannot escape and is forced to engage Beowulf on the Geat's terms: a wrestling match, where his great strength and strong grip afford him the best chance of victory.

The violence of the struggle between Beowulf and Grendel nearly brings down the hall. The other Geats in the hall leap up to aid Beowulf but are unable to injure Grendel with their weapons because "no blade on earth, no blacksmith's art could ever damage their demon opponent."[xvi] No matter what Grendel does, he cannot overpower Beowulf, nor can he escape the arm lock. Beowulf has Grendel right where he wants him and refuses to let go:

> The monster's whole body was in pain, a tremendous wound appeared on his shoulder. Sinews split and the bone lappings burst.[xvii]

Beowulf's wrenching grip is so strong that he dislocates Grendel's shoulder and rips it from the socket. Grendel loses his arm but is able to escape the hall. He is mortally wounded and returns to his desolate lair in the fens and swamplands to die.

The next day, the Danes return to the hall. They see Grendel's tracks and the trail of blood he left when he returned to his liar. They also see Grendel's arm and shoulder "displayed high up near the roof: the whole of Grendel's shoulder and arms, his awesome grasp."[xviii] They immediately realize Grendel has been defeated and they need no longer live in terror of the creature. All the Danes, including Unferth, rejoice over Beowulf's victory; they celebrate with sporting contests and a huge feast, in which there is a great deal of eating and drinking, and a poem about a blood feud between two kingdoms is recited within the larger *Beowulf* poem. None of the Danes or Geats seems aware that Grendel has a family nor did they consider how the bloody display of Grendel's arm might affect his kinsman. That night, the Danes bed down in the hall after eating and drinking:

> At their heads they placed their polished timber battle shields, and on the bench above them, each man's kit was kept to hand: a towering war-helmet, webbed mail shirt and great shafted spear. It was their habit always and everywhere to be ready for action.[xix]

The Danes have learned nothing. They prepare for conventional enemies but even after encountering one monster, they do not even consider the possibility that there may be more of them in the area. As a result of this lack of imagination, things take a turn for the worse for the Danes.

Grendel's mother is "grief-wracked and ravenous, desperate for revenge" after the death of her son. She visits Heorot the night after the battle, using the same tactics her son employed, slinking in unobserved under cover of darkness. She devours a thane named Aeschere, who is a counselor and a beloved personal friend of Hrothgar. The Danes then wake in terror and grab their swords and shields, although the helmets and chain mail are useless because there is no time to put them on. Grendel's mother is a formidable opponent, but no match for all of the alerted Danes. She is "in a panic, desperate to get out, in mortal terror", but before she leaves, she grabs Grendel's arm, which had been displayed as a trophy, and escapes back into the night. [xx]

Hrothgar is distraught to find he is still not free from attack. He and some of his fellow Danes seem to despair, but Beowulf tells them it "is always better to avenge dear ones that to indulge in mourning" [xxi] and offers to pursue and fight Grendel's mother. The Danes are encouraged, and their spirits revive from Beowulf's words. Unferth, who had previously questioned and criticized Beowulf, does everything he can do to help, going so far as giving Beowulf his family's ancestral sword, Hrunting, to help him defeat Grendel's mother. The Danes and Geats track Grendel to his lair. They soon come to a "dismal wood, above grey stones...the bloodshot water surged underneath." Any uncertainty they may have about where to look in order to find Grendel's mother is removed when they find Aeschere's head lying next to the foot of the cliff on the shores of a foul body of water. There are "writhing sea dragons and monsters slouching on the slopes by the cliff...hot gore kept wallowing up...the water was infested with all kinds of reptiles." Beowulf does not say anything. Instead, he dispatches one of the creatures with the "seasoned shaft" of an arrow from his bow. [xxii] He then:

> Got ready, donned his war gear, indifferent to death; his mighty hand-forged, fine-webbed mail... to guard his head he had a glittering helmet... and another item lent by Unferth... a hilted weapon... a rare and ancient sword named Hrunting....[xxiii]

Beowulf then plunges into the water. His extraordinary swimming skills allow him to dive down in full armor. Grendel's mother, "that swamp thing from hell, the tarn-hag in all her terrible strength," lurks at the bottom of the mere, where she senses that Beowulf is coming near. She lunges and manages to catch him, but is unable to injure him due to the protection of the chain mail. She drags Beowulf down to "her court," a sort of air-filled cave or enclosure underneath the water. Beowulf immediately swings Hrunting into action so that it is "ringing and singing" on the head of Grendel's mother, but the blade is "unable to bite." Beowulf tosses the sword away and tries to kill his opponent with his bare hands.

He throws her to the floor of the underground cavern, but she leaps up and gets a grip on Beowulf, who stumbles and falls to the ground. She pulls out a broad, whetted knife and tries to plunge it into Beowulf, but his chain mail turns the blade and saves his life. Beowulf struggles back to his feet and sees an ancient sword on the wall. It is a huge sword, far too heavy for most men to lift, but the Geat hero is able to pick it up and strike Grendel's mother. The weapon bites "deep into her neck bone... and severed it entirely, toppling the doomed house of flesh." Beowulf has fought and killed another monster. Beowulf then inspects the cavern further and finds the body of Grendel, which he decapitates. The blade of the ancient weapon then begins to "wilt into gory icicles" and melts away completely. He explores further and sees enormous treasure, but he takes none of it. He takes only Hrunting, the head of Grendel, and the hilt of the ancient blade he found in the cave when he swims back to the surface.

The entire battle beneath the surface of the bog lasts nine hours. The men waiting for Beowulf see blood mixed in with a surge in the waves, but they have no idea what is going below the surface. The Danes eventually leave. The Geats do not leave: instead they wait and wish, "without hope, to behold their lord, Beowulf himself." When Beowulf arrives at the surface his loyal companions rejoice and are overjoyed to see him.

The Geats return to Heorot with the massive head of Grendel and the hilt of the ancient sword. Beowulf tells Hrothgar and his court about the hard-fought battle with Grendel's mother, attributing his victory to divine intervention that allowed him to see the ancient sword on the wall. He declares, "…Danes never need you fear for a single thane of your sept or nation, young warriors or old, that laying waste of life that you and your people endured of yore." [xxiv] Hrothgar has yet another celebration, even greater than the first. He is very grateful to Beowulf for all that he has done, but he does give the hero warning:

> Almighty God in His magnificence favors our race with rank and scope and the gift of wisdom; his sway is wide. Sometimes He allows the mind of man of distinguished birth to follow its bent, grants him fulfillment and felicity on earth and forts to command in his own country. He permits him to lord it in many lands until the man in his unthinkingness forgets that it will ever end for him. He indulges his desires, illness and old age seem nothing to him; his mind is untroubled by envy or malice or the thought of enemies with their hate-honed swords. The whole world

conforms to his will; he is kept from the worst until an element of overweening enters him and takes hold… Choose, dear Beowulf, the better part… do not give way to pride. For a brief while your strength is in blood but it fades quickly; and soon there will follow illness or the sword to lay you low… and death will arrive, dear warrior, to sweep you away…[xxv]

Beowulf thanks Unferth for the use of his sword, even though it was not the weapon he ultimately used to kill Grendel's mother. Hrothgar gives many expensive gifts to Beowulf, and he departs from the Danes a hero.

When Beowulf returns home, he immediately reports to his lord, King Hygalec, and gives an account of himself. He also gives some of the treasure he received from Hrothgar to Hygalec, who reciprocates by giving Beowulf gifts that include land, cattle, and a hall of his own. When Hygalec dies, Beowulf continues to serve his son. Finally, when the son dies and there is no heir, Beowulf is made king. He rules the kingdom of the Geats wisely for 50 years, until he suddenly faces one last battle. A slave or servant "fleeing the hand" [xxvi] of a cruel master takes shelter in a crevice in the rocks and accidently discovers he has found a barrow left over from some ancient, lost people who died off hundreds of years ago. The barrow contains a huge treasure hoard. The man takes a single golden cup from all the treasure, returns home, and offers it to his master in the hope of being forgiven and treated better in the future.

The barrow contains more than just treasure. There is also a sleeping dragon, awakened by the trespasser. He immediately notices the missing cup, as well as the foot-prints of the man who stole it. The dragon is enraged, and when night falls he attacks the local farmers who had nothing to do with the cruel master and his runaway slave. The terrifying creature:

> rippled down the rock, writhing with anger when he saw the footprints of the prowler who had sto-len too close to his dreaming head... The hoard guardian scorched the ground as he scoured and hunted for the trespasser who had troubled his sleep. Hot and savage, he kept circling and cir-cling the outside of the mound. No man appeared in that desert waste, but he worked himself up by imagining battle; then back in he'd go in search of the cup... So the guardian of the mound, the hoard-watcher, waited for the gloaming with fierce impatience; his pent-up fury at the loss of the ves-sel made him long to hit back and lash out in flames. Then, to his delight, the day waned and he could wait no longer behind the wall, but hurtled forth in a fiery blaze. The first to suffer were the people on the land... The dragon began to belch out flames and burn bright homesteads; there was a hot glow that scared everyone, for the vile sky-winger would leave nothing alive in his wake.... Far and near, the Geat nation bore the brunt of his brutal assaults and virulent hate. Then back to the hoard he would dart before daybreak, to hide in his den... Then Beowulf was given bad news, a hard truth: his own home, the best of buildings, had been burnt to a cinder... [xxvii]

The news of the dragon's predations and the destruction of his own home temporarily paralyze Beowulf with despair. Like Hrothgar many years ago, he wonders if and how he has somehow inadvertently offended God and brought the dragon upon the kingdom as a punishment.

Even in his old age, Beowulf is a great warrior. He rouses himself to action and devises a plan to fight and defeat the dragon. He orders a special fireproof iron shield to be made for use against his opponent. He is "too proud to line up a large army" [xxviii] against the dragon. Instead, he and eleven comrades compel the thief who stole the cup to guide them to the barrow. [xxix] When they arrive at the barrow Beowulf feels unsettled and sad, somehow sensing his imminent demise. He tells his companions:

> As king of the people I shall pursue this fight for the glory of winning… men at arms, remain here on the barrow, safe in your amour. This fight is not yours, nor is it up to any man except me to measure his strength against the monster or to prove his worth. I shall win the gold by my courage, or else mortal combat, doom of battle, will bear your lord away. [xxx]

After these words he "gave a shout" [xxxi] and advanced down the path into the barrow. The "hoard-guard" awakes and is enraged by this shouted challenge, and so "roused to fury, each antagonist strikes terror in the other." [xxxii] The dragon blasts Beowulf with flame. Beowulf uses his iron shield to protect himself and slashes at the dragon with so much force that his blade shatters. He is unable to penetrate the creature's scales and is forced to give ground, perhaps for the first time in his life. Meanwhile, Beowulf's companions watch the struggle and see the advancing dragon. Tragically:

> No help or backing was to be had then from his high-born comrades; that hand-picked troop broke ranks and ran for their lives to the safety of the wood. But within one heart sorrow welled up in a man of worth… His name was Wiglaf… Sad at heart, addressing his comrades, Wiglaf spoke wise and fluent words: 'I remember that time when mead was flowing, how we pledged loyalty to our lord in the hall, promising our ring-giver [Beowulf] we would be worth our price, make good the gift of the war gear, those swords and helmets, as and when he required it. He picked out from the army deliberately, honoured us and judged us fit for this action, and all because he considered us the best of his arms-bearing thanes. And now, although he wanted this challenge to be one he'd face alone… now the day has come when this lord we serve needs sound men to give him their support. Let us go to him, help our leader through the hot flame and dread of fire… I would rather my body were robed in the same burning blaze as my gold-giver's body than go back bearing arms. That is unthinkable, unless we have first slain the foe and defended the life of the Weather-Geats… We must bond together, shield and helmet, mail-shirt and sword…" [xxxiii]

After speaking these words to his comrades, Wiglaf, who is not only one of Beowulf's warriors but also a distant relative, wades into the fight. The dragon sees him coming, becomes further enraged, and attacks again. His fire quickly consumes Wiglaf's wooden shield; Wiglaf then hides behind Beowulf's iron shield. Beowulf is "inspired again by the thought of glory" xxxiv and delivers a sword stroke to the dragon's skull. The creature bites Beowulf in the neck but in so doing exposes himself, and Wiglaf stabs the beast in the belly. The wound does not kill the dragon, but the creature can no longer produce flame. Beowulf reaches for a hunting knife in his belt and delivers a mortal wound to the dragon. The Geat hero has killed another monster.

After the battle, Beowulf feels himself growing weaker. He asks Wiglaf to bring out the treasure from the barrow so that he can see it. Wiglaf hurries to do so, fearing that by the time he has gathered up all the treasure and brought it to the surface the old king will be dead. When Wiglaf returns to the surface, Beowulf looks sadly at it, then speaks:

> To everlasting Lord of All, to the King of Glory, I give thanks that I behold this treasure here before me that I have been allowed to leave my people so well-endowed on the day I die. Now that I have bartered my last breath to own this fortune, it is up to you to look to their needs. I can hold out no longer. Order my troop to construct a barrow on a head lance on the coast, after my pyre has cooled. It will loom in the horizon at Hroneness and be a reminder among my people—so that in

coming times crews under sail will call it Beowulf's
Barrow as they steer across the wide and shrouded
waters. Then the king in his great-heartedness un-
clasped the collar of gold from his neck and gave
it to the young thane, telling him to use it and the
warshirt and the gilded helmet well. "You are the
last of us, the only one left of the Waegmundings.
Fate swept us away, sent my whole brave high-
born clan to their final doom. Now I must follow
them…" xxxv

His final request is to continue to be honored and also
to serve others with the barrow dedicated to him along
the coast that will commemorate his achievements and
also help to guide mariners through the local waters.

When the cowardly thanes finally emerge from the
forest and approach the barrow, they find Wiglaf kneel-
ing by the body of Beowulf, "sitting worn out, a comrade
shoulder to shoulder with his lord, trying in vain to bring
him round with water." xxxvi Wiglaf looks at the men with
disdain and disappointment. He rebukes them for their
hypocrisy of accepting gifts from Beowulf in return for
pledge of loyalty, then running and hiding when Beowulf
needed them most:

Anyone ready to admit the truth will surely realize
that the lord of men who showered you with gifts
and gave you the armor you are standing in—
when he would distribute helmets and mail shirts
to men on the mead-benches, a prince treating
his thanes in hall to the best he could find far or
near—was throwing weapons uselessly away. xxxvii

Wiglaf then predicts that once other nations, such as the Swedes, hear of their cowardice, dishonor, and the breakdown of their ranks, they will be emboldened to attack the Geats:

> Nor do I expect peace or pact-keeping of any sort from the Swedes…they will cross our borders and attack in force when they find out Beowulf is dead… Such is the drift of the dire report that the gallant man delivered. He got little wrong in what he told and predicted. xxxviii

Wiglaf and the other Geats take a last look at Beowulf, lying side by side with the dragon. He observes:

> Often when one man follows his own will many are hurt. This happened to us. Nothing we advised could ever convince the prince we loved, our land's guardian, not to vex the custodian of the gold [the dragon], let him lie where he was long accustomed, lurk there under the earth until the end of the world. He held to his high destiny. The hoard is laid bare, but at a grave cost: it was too cruel a fate that forced the king to that encounter. xxxix

The Geats carry out Beowulf's dying wish. They cremate him and build a barrow to his memory. The poem ends with a summary of Beowulf's life:

> So the Geat people, his hearth companions, sorrowed for the Lord who had been laid low. They said of all the kings on earth, he was the man most gracious and fair-minded, kindest to his people and keenest to win fame.[xl]

The audiences who heard or read this poem ten centuries ago were left with a lot to ponder afterward. They may have wondered things, like did Beowulf really live? Did Grendel really exist? Is there such a thing as a dragon? Are we at risk of being attacked by other dragons? Some other subtler questions may have also come to their minds. For example, they may have wondered if Hrothgar was really a good military and political leader, or was he foolish to build Heorot, thereby antagonizing Grendel? Was he weak or incompetent because he was unable to stop Grendel's predations on his people? Could Beowulf have returned the cup the frightened man had stolen from the dragon's hoard and thus avoided the battle that resulted in his death? Or would this act of appeasement not have done him or the Geats any good? Was Unferth right about Beowulf being a brash and foolish man, one who was so fixated on his own personal glory that he recklessly decided to have a swimming contest with Breca as a youth, nearly getting both of them drowned, and then at the end of his life chose to fight the dragon alone, thereby getting himself killed and leaving his kingdom leaderless? Should Beowulf have asked for help from his warriors to defeat the dragon? Why did his companions help him when he fought Grendel, but then, with the exception of Wiglaf, abandon him when he fought the dragon? An examination of these questions teaches us a lot about the poem Beowulf and maybe even a little bit about ourselves.

CHAPTER 2
Hrothgar and the Danes: The Conventional Warfighters

Hrothgar is a king with "courage and greatness." [xli] He is a generous, charismatic leader. He attracts so many followers to his banner that he soon has a mighty army of "Spear Danes." He expands upon his forefathers' conquests and is able to "establish sway over all the rich strongholds" [xlii] around the central core of his ancestors' kingdom. But, Hrothgar is not simply a "wrecker of mead benches" like his great grandfather Shield Sheafson, or a "defender of the forts" like his grandfather Beow. He is also a "friend of the people." [xliii] He and his fellow Danes are building a new society capable of defending itself militarily, building fortifications, and constructing infrastructure for travel and trade, such as the paved track Beowulf and his companions use to travel from the coast to Heorot. The pinnacle of their efforts is construction of the great hall:

> Meant to be a wonder of the world forever; it would be his throne-room and there he would dispense his God given goods to young and old— but not the common land or people's lives...[xliv]

He spares no expense in building the hall, and when it is completed it is a symbol of the wealth, prosperity, and sophistication of Hrothgar and the Danes flourishing under his leadership. They have built a magnificent hall from which their king rules, dispensing justice, giving gifts, and holding wonderful celebrations. The story of the Spear Danes parallels the story of the people of Scandinavia and Northern Europe who migrated to Britain after the collapse of the Roman Empire and slowly created a new civilization. The story of Hrothgar and the Spear Danes is a story about the creation of civil society and nation-building.

The poem leaves no doubt that Hrothgar can lead the Danes, with their armor, swords, and other heavy weaponry, to victory in battle against any conventional foe. However, Hrothgar is at a loss as to how to fight such an unconventional enemy as Grendel. He has very little knowledge, or what we might call actionable intelligence, on the creature, even after suffering from the terror of his attacks for twelve years. He does not know where Grendel lives, and it is only about halfway through the poem that Hrothgar says, "I have heard it said by people in my hall, counselors who live in the upland country, that they have seen two such creatures [like Grendel] prowling the moors, huge marauders from some other world." [xlv] This information about the numbers and behavior of Grendel and his kind is very useful information, yet Hrothgar fails to mention it to Beowulf until after Grendel's mother has struck and killed a man.

Hrothgar has what we might call a successful administration, at least up until the predations of Grendel begin on his people. The creature is a disaster for Hrothgar. His "household-guard are on the wane, fate sweeps them away into Grendel's clutches." [xlvi] On a more personal level, these are "hard times, heart-breaking for the prince of

Shieldings." [xlvii] In desperation he makes offerings to pagan idols, but no help comes as a result. Hrothgar cannot defend his kingdom against Grendel, and the creature's small but steady attacks, spread out over a period of many years, cause both a logistical and a literal hemorrhaging of warriors that slowly drains the military manpower of his kingdom, weakening and demoralizing Hrothgar and his people, who must abandon the hall they built every night out of fear of their unconventional enemy.

Hrothgar's battle with an unconventional enemy who employs guerrilla tactics would have been a familiar situation to the Anglo-Saxon audience. There is ample documentation that the Britons, as well as the Goths and other Northern European tribes, used guerrilla warfare against the Romans and against each other. [xlviii] The poem depicts a situation little different from the one that our own contemporary leaders find themselves in as they struggle against unconventional enemies who employ terror to achieve their goals.

Westerners tend to think that conventional conflicts, involving large armies that employ enormous firepower to slaughter each other in brief, decisive battles, have been the dominant form of conflict in human history. In fact, they are relatively rare in the history of conflict, if only because most societies have not had the resources to support such large military forces. Martin Van Creveld, in *The Transformation of War,* which was published in 1991, estimates that from 1945 until the time that he wrote the book there had been about 160 armed conflicts in the world. About 75% of these conflicts were what he terms "low-intensity conflicts." He argues that there are three essential features that define a low-intensity conflict. The first is that they tend to take place in less-developed parts of the world; if they do take place in more modernized societies, they tend to be called something besides a war or conflict, like terrorism. The second feature is that these conflicts rarely involve regular uniformed troops fighting on both sides. Instead, at least one side of the conflict employs fighters who may be guerillas, terrorists, civilians, or other unorthodox combatants. Third, most low-intensity conflicts involve at least some combatants who do not rely on airplanes, submarines, tanks or other complicated, expensive weapons systems. These low intensity conflicts have been the most prevalent form of warfare since 1945.

Conventional twentieth century military forces, even when armed with sophisticated, state of the art, weapons, lost to unconventional enemies in Indochina, Algiers, and Afghanistan. Van Creveld concludes that "the cold brutal fact is that much present-day military power is simply irrelevant as an instrument for extending or defending political interests over most of the globe; by this criterion, indeed, it scarcely amounts to military power at all." [xlix]

Hrothgar's struggle with Grendel fulfills all three of the criteria Van Creveld uses to define a low-intensity conflict. It takes place in a small, remote, newly established kingdom, and Grendel frequents the moors, or upland country, which would have been marginal lands, unsuited for farming and a place that would be difficult for an army to maneuver and fight in. The Danish warriors are readily identified as combatants by their weapons and armor, but Grendel does not wear any identifying uniform. The Danes are technologically superior to Grendel, employing edged metal weapons in battle, whereas Grendel has nothing but his own physical strength. The first part of this ancient poem describes a conflict between the conventional Danish warriors and an unconventional enemy, and just as in most actual conflicts of the modern age, the conventional war-fighters are losing.

America has fought many unconventional enemies in her history, most recently in Vietnam, Iraq, and Afghanistan. The American strategy in Vietnam under General Westmorland was a straightforward one. U.S. military forces were deployed to protect bases along the coast and around Saigon. At the same time, forces were placed in the central highlands to prevent the North Vietnamese from advancing across the country from the west to the coast, for that would cut the country in half and disrupt American and South Vietnamese operations and control. Westmorland's plan was to launch a series of "search and destroy" missions, where American forces with enormous firepower would sweep through the country, searching out and engaging North Vietnamese and other forces hostile to the forces of Southern Vietnam and crushing them with superior firepower.

In conjunction with this plan, there was to be simultaneous bombing of North Vietnam. The entire plan was predicated on the use of overwhelming amounts of brute force. The people of South Vietnam would be persuaded to support the U.S.-supported South Vietnamese government because, as U.S. soldiers said at the time, if you "grab them by the balls their hearts and minds will follow." [1] The use of force was focused primarily on seeking out and destroying the enemy. It left the people unprotected and did not address the social, economic, and political problems that plagued South Vietnam. The people did not appreciate the incursion of foreign troops in their country, and the inability of Americans and the South Vietnamese government to create a civil society with some sort of security, rule of law, and economic prosperity drove the population into supporting North Vietnamese. For every enemy the U.S. military killed, it created many more by alienating the people. Eventually, the cost in blood and treasure became too much for Americans to bear, and after about 10 or 12 years of fighting, the U.S. withdrew from Vietnam. A few years later, the North Vietnamese overthrew the government of South Vietnam to become the sole rulers of all of Vietnam. Hrothgar and his heavily armed troops would have immediately grasped Westmorland's plan to use overwhelming force to crush the enemy. Unfortunately, both Hrothgar and Westmorland had an elusive enemy that fought in an unconventional manner. The duration of the conflict between Hrothgar and Grendel is twelve years. The United States was involved militarily in Vietnam in some form or another for about ten or twelve years. Hrothgar and his people are on the verge of despair after the long years of Grendel's terror. In fact, Hrothgar almost seems to decompensate emotionally when he learns Grendel's mother has visited the hall and killed Aeschere, one of his most trusted and beloved thanes. Only after reassuring words from Beowulf is he able to collect himself and help lead Beowulf and his Geat companions through the moor to the lake where Grendel and his mother live. Similarly, the Vietnam War was a terrible, traumatic experience for the American psyche. It led to the collapse of Lyndon Johnson's presidency and his decision not to seek reelection in 1968. As a result of the Vietnam War, many Americans concluded that the United States is incapable of fighting a low-intensity conflict against an unconventional enemy.

A longer view of history reveals that, actually, the United States has fought and defeated many formidable unconventional enemies. Americans defeated an insurgency in the Philippines that arose after the Spanish American War. Americans also fought and won against the Huk insurgency, which was also in the Philippines in the 1950's, as well as the insurgents in the Greek civil war immediately after World War II. [li] These victories were won through a combination of conventional military forces, unconventional military forces, and efforts to create a civil society that provided a better alternative for the population than the one offered by the insurgents.

Hrothgar realizes he cannot defeat Grendel with his conventional forces. He is desperate and willing to accept aid from anyone, including foreign fighters. Many heroes before Beowulf came to spend the night in Heorot to fight Grendel, but they were all dead by morning. Hrothgar does not give up. He eventually finds the right man for the job in Beowulf. This is not so different from the situation in which America found itself in Iraq. In early 2003, the United States launched a campaign using sophisticated weapons to defeat Saddam Hussein and his Baathist regime. The American military used conventional forces to apply massive firepower against the Iraqis; within a few weeks their army disintegrated and Saddam was in hiding.

On May 1, 2003, President George Bush declared "the end of major conflict." It may have been the end of major conventional battles, but nobody told the enemy that it was the end of major conflict. A new enemy, a sort of amalgam of remnants of Baathist supporters, Al-Qaeda, and Shiite groups emerged and continued to fight, but in a very different way than Saddam's army had. They

employed stealth and surprise, relying heavily on impro-
vised explosive devices to kill and maim U.S. forces, as
well as kidnapping, assassination, and other acts of terrorism to control the Iraqi population. By 2006 Al-Qaeda
controlled much of the country.

George Bush was desperate. He decided to change his
strategy and give the command of his forces to an expert in
counterinsurgency and unconventional warfare: General
David Petreus. Amidst widespread skepticism not dissim-
ilar to Unferth's doubts about Beowulf, General Petreus
took control of the U.S. military and implemented a
counterinsurgency strategy that relied not only on conventional forces but also unconventional forces, as well
as a civil affairs program to improve the lives of ordinary
Iraqis. Within two years the tide of war changed, and U.S.
and Iraqi government forces had killed or captured most
of Al-Qaeda and other guerrilla forces in Iraq, resulting
in the decline in the level of violence and the growth of a
new civil society. [lii]

Passions in America still run high about the Vietnam
War, and the emotions are so intense about the Iraq
War that oftentimes when Americans try to talk about
it, the discussions break down into screaming matches.
It may or may not be true that President Johnson and
President Bush were bad presidents. It may or may not be
true that they were good presidents. It is true that both
men learned what the Russians learned in Afghanistan,
what the French learned in Algeria, and what Hrothgar
realized in *Beowulf*: it is difficult, if not impossible, for
conventional military forces to fight and win against a determined, unconventional enemy.

CHAPTER 3
Grendel and His Clan: The Insurgents

Grendel does not speak a single word in *Beowulf*. In spite of this, we learn a great deal about him from the narrator of the poem. He is described thus:

> grim demon haunting the marches, marauding round the heath and the desolate fens; he had dwelt for a time in misery among the banished monsters, Cain's clan, whom the creator had outlawed and condemned as outcasts. For the killing Abel the Eternal Lord had exacted a price: Cain got no good from committing that murder because the Almighty made him anathema and out of the curse of his exile there sprang ogres and elves and evil phantoms...[liii]

The poem introduces Grendel to the audience the same way it introduces Hrothgar, by telling us about his family and where he came from. Grendel is a descendant of Cain. The Bible tells us that Adam and Eve had two sons. Cain "worked the soil;" he was a farmer. The other son, Abel, "kept the flocks," or was a shepherd. They both decided to make a sacrifice to God, even though it is nowhere stated that God asked them to do so. Cain's offering consisted of the "fruits of the soil," presumably grains and vegetables. Abel offered up the "fat portions from some of the firstborn of his flock," or a lamb.

God was more pleased with Abel's offering than with Cain's offering. The Bible never tells us why. Cain became wildly angry and jealous of his brother. In a fit of passion, he murdered Abel. After the murder, God asked Cain a rhetorical question: "Where is your brother?" Cain responded to the question with the question, "am I my brother's keeper?" God answered Cain's question with the statement that Abel's blood cried out from the ground out to him that he had been murdered. As a result of this murder, God placed a mark on Cain's forehead, and he was driven out of Eden. [liv]

Cain went on to found a city and a dynasty in the land of Nod. His descendants were proud, strong, and violent. One of Cain's descendants, named Lamach, boasted, "I have slain a man to my wounding and a young man to my bruising. If Cain shall be avenged sevenfold, truly Lamach seventy and sevenfold." It is not exactly clear what Lamach meant by this statement. Scholars have argued that either Lamach took fatal revenge on men who merely wounded or bruised him, or his strength was so great that he could easily and effortlessly strike a man dead with one blow. Whatever the exact meaning of the passage of Scripture, it is clear that Cain's descendant Lamach was no one to trifle with. [lv] Because Grendel is a descendant of Cain, the audience immediately knows he and his kin are violent, dangerous outlaws, condemned to banishment from birth.

The poem never states how long Grendel has roamed the moors and uplands of Hrothgar's kingdom, but it does say Grendel's mother has lived in the area for "a hundred seasons." [lvi] If each generation of Spear Danes is about 20 years, then the time from the arrival of Shield Sheafson to the time of the kingship of Beow, then Halfdane, and finally Hrothgar is only about 60 to 80 years. According to the chronology outlined in the poem, Grendel and his clan may have been in the area longer than the Spear Danes, and certainly longer than the existence of Heorot. We are also told that Grendel and his mother are not alone. There are other descendants of Cain who "dwell apart among wolves on the hills, on windswept crags and treacherous keshes, where cold streams pour down the mountain and disappear under mist and moorland." [lvii]

We never learn why Grendel lives in the swamplands. It may be that literature is echoing actual historical events in which the Anglo-Saxons, newly arrived in Britain from Scandinavia and Northern Europe, pushed the indigenous populations from the more desirable farming and grazing lands into the swamps and other marginal areas. These are areas where Hrothgar and his Spear Danes in the poem, like the real life Anglo-Saxons who heard the poem a millennia ago, could have been literally bogged down by heavy armor and weapons if they tried to move around, where a more lightly armed, mobile opponent, would have enjoyed a relative advantage, even if they possessed less sophisticated weapons. The relationship between events in the poem and real life are speculative. However, rugged terrain, mountains, swamps, and heavy vegetation generally favor unconventional war-fighters, in part because it neutralizes many of the advantages in firepower conventional military forces may have. [lviii]

They may be the descendants of Cain, but Grendel and his clan still feel pain, and they still feel affection for one another. Grendel's mother is "grief-wracked" [lix] by the sight of the mutilated body of her dead son in her cave. She goes to Heorot the night after Grendel's battle with Beowulf, looking for revenge, another eminently human emotion. She encounters several Spear Danes sleeping in the hall. She, like Grendel, is enormously strong, and kills the warrior Aeschere in his sleep. When other warriors are awakened by the noise and in terror grab their swords and shields to defend themselves, Grendel's mother is outnumbered, and "in a panic, desperate to get out" she "snatches their trophy, Grendel's bloodied hand: [lx] and then escapes to the fen. Grendel and his clan may look different from the Spear Danes, but they experience the same emotions, like fear and grief, and the same motivations, like revenge, drive their actions.

Just as Cain had a homicidal rage directed toward his brother Abel, Grendel nurses a "hard grievance" [lxi] against Hrothgar and the Spear Danes. He hates the disturbing "din of the loud banquet every day in the hall, the harp being struck and the clear song of the skilled poet telling with mastery of man's beginnings." He decides to wage a "lonely war" [lxii] against Hrothgar and his people by entering the Hall, the symbol of the Hrothgar's civilization, and then "inflicting cruelties on the people... atrocious hurt... raids at night." [lxiii] Grendel never engages the Spear Danes out in the open or during the day, when they could mass their forces against him. His use of stealth, the element of surprise, the avoidance of a conventional, pitched battle with the Spear Danes, and the desecration of bodies are all tactics of an unconventional war-fighter to inspire terror in an enemy. *Beowulf* is the first great poem of the English language, and Grendel is the first terrorist insurgent in English literature.

Words like low-intensity conflict, insurgency, and terrorism are widely used but poorly defined terms. Low-intensity conflicts can take many forms. They can manifest as an insurrection or a rebellion, where a group of revolutionaries tries to overthrow a government by means of an uprising of a population against the government. There is no evidence in the poem that Grendel is trying to inspire the Spear Danes or his fellow members of the clan of Cain to overthrow Hrothgar. Another form of low-intensity conflict is a guerrilla war. Again, there is no evidence in the poem that any members of Grendel's clan are in conflict with the Spear Danes besides Grendel. Grendel's mother does not seem to have any quarrel with the Danes until her son is killed by Beowulf and his arm hung from the rafters as a gory trophy.

Terrorism is another form of low-intensity conflict. One goal of the terrorist is to inflict such a high cost in blood and treasure on a government that it eventually agrees to give in to the demands of the terrorist. Grendel only attacks individuals in the hall; these men would have been the most prominent warriors in the employ of Hrothgar. These are men like Aeschere, who we learn is very close to Hrothgar. They are the men the king depends on to rule his kingdom and defend it from enemies. There is no mention in the poem of him attacking anyone else, like local farmers or ordinary subjects under the rule of Hrothgar. Grendel is using terrorism to decapitate the Danish kingdom's leadership, forcing Hrothgar and his forces to abandon Heorot, at least after dark. This is a blow to the power and prestige of Hrothgar and the Spear Danes, thus a victory for Grendel.

In the twelve years that the creature conducts his campaign of terror, he transforms Heorot from a symbol of hope and light for a new society into one of death and defeat. In spite of all of this, he is not able to muster an attack that will definitely defeat Hrothgar. There is no evidence in the poem that any of the Danes consider abandoning Hrothgar. There is also no indication that Grendel could persuade any other member of the Clan of Cain to join him in his fight against Hrothgar and his people. There is no indication that Grendel and his clan have any sort of civil society that rivals Hrothgar and Heorot hall. Grendel may be a good terrorist, but he lives a miserable life.

Terror is not something found just in *Beowulf*. It is part of our world as well. The United States is now in conflict with an enemy, Al-Qaeda, that embraces terror. Just as Grendel focused his attacks on the people who spent the night in Heorot, the symbol of Danish civilization, Al-Qaeda attacked the Twin Towers, symbols of American wealth and power, on September 11. 2001. When America defeated Saddam's conventional military forces in 2003 and then proceeded to disband the government and the army, it failed to replace these institutions with anything that could guarantee a society that provided safety and prosperity for ordinary Iraqis. Al-Qaeda saw its chance. It presented itself to Iraqis as a group of defenders who would liberate Iraq from Americans. By 2004 Al-Qaeda was strong enough to capture and kill several American contractors and hang their charred bodies from a bride in Fallujah, promising many more dead Americans in the future unless its demands were met. Al-Qaeda, like Grendel, is good at terrorism.

Al-Qaeda is also like Grendel in that it is unable to create a civil society that fulfills the needs of ordinary people. Michael Yon, in his book *Moment of Truth in Iraq* writes:

> Once they [Al-Qaeda] have gained control of and responsibility for a territory, they can offer only terror. They do not know or care how to run a village, much less a city or a nation. The locals came to view Al-Qaeda as degenerates and swine—using drugs, laying up sloppy drunk, using prostitutes, raping women and boys, and cutting off heads. [lxiv]

The insurgents in Iraq were able to use terror to prevent U.S. and coalition forces from creating a civil society that met the needs of the Iraqi people, but they were unable to defeat the U.S. for the same reason that Grendel could kill Danish warriors, making Hrothgar look weak and impotent, but could not defeat the Danes. Both Grendel and Al-Qaeda are unable to provide for the needs of the people. They only "know how to kill people and break things…that's where their skill set ends." [lxv] If insurgents can inflict terror on a conventional enemy, then they cannot be defeated, but if they cannot offer people the hope of a new society that is better than the one they are fighting against, they cannot win. The result is a stalemate that can last for years, like the one described in *Beowulf.* Hrothgar is truly a good king, because even though he realizes he is unable to defeat his unconventional enemy, he does not despair. He does not give up. He gives a warfighter with expertise in unconventional conflicts the opportunity to fight Grendel.

CHAPTER 4
Beowulf and His Companions: The Counterinsurgents

The poem introduces Beowulf to the audience the same way it introduces Hrothgar and Grendel, by telling us about his forefathers. He is the son of a "famous man...a noble warrior"[lxvi] named Ecgtheow, who married the sister of King Hygelac. Beowulf comes from a reputable family, but one that is far less distinguished than Hrothgar's and less notorious than Grendel's. Beowulf was:

> poorly regarded for a long time, was taken by the Geats for less than he was worth: and their Lord [Hygelac] too had never much esteemed him in the mead-hall. They firmly believed that he lacked force...[lxvii]

He comports himself in a meek and mild-mannered fashion, at least in comparison to other medieval Vikings, but he impresses people with his physical size and strength.[lxviii] The watchman who guards the coast of Hrothgar's kingdom and meets Beowulf and his fellow Geats when they arrive on the shore takes a look at Beowulf and tells him he has never "seen a mightier man-at-arms on this earth than the one standing here: unless I am mistaken, he is truly noble. This is no mere hanger-on in a hero's armour."[lxix] The watchman allows the Geats to proceed unmolested to Hrothgar's court. When they arrive at the court they meet one of Hrothgar's officers, who says that he has never seen "so impressive or large an assembly of strangers. Stoutness of heart, bravery not banishment, must have brought you to Hrothgar." [lxx] Later, Wulfgar, a tribal chief at Hrothgar's court, tells the king Beowulf and his fellow Geats would like an audience with him. Wulfgar observes "from their arms and appointment, they appear well born and worthy of respect, especially the one who has led them this far: he is formidable indeed." [lxxi] Neither the coastal watchman nor the men at Heorot have ever met or heard of Beowulf before he arrives in Hrothgar's kingdom. They know nothing of his lineage or his family reputation. All they know comes from what they can see with their own eyes, and Beowulf looks like a helluva war-fighter to them.

Upon hearing his men's description of the visitor, Hrothgar immediately knows it is Beowulf. The Danish King explains that he was told by a crew of seamen who sailed for him to the land of the Geats years ago about "a thane... with the strength of thirty in the grip of each hand." [lxxii] Hrothgar also knows that Beowulf's family owes him a debt because he protected Ecgtheow from danger during one of the constant tribal wars many years ago. Everyone in the Danish court knows any man who can kill Grendel and rid the kingdom of this scourge will win fame and fortune.

When Beowulf finally makes his physical entrance into Heorot and meets Hrothgar, he greets the king, identifies himself, and states the purpose of his visit: to kill Grendel. He then goes on to give a sort of resume of his experiences that make him qualified to fight and kill Grendel:

Been bolstered in the blood of enemies when I
battled and bound five beasts, raided a troll nest
and in the night sea slaughtered sea brutes. I have
suffered extremes and avenged the Geats (their
enemies brought it upon themselves, I devastated
them). lxxiii

This resume is very unlike that of Shield Sheafson, who
is described as a "terror of the hall troops." lxxiv Or that of
Beow, who defended the forts. lxxv Or that of Hrothgar,
who was the leader of a large army. Beowulf is not a king
or prince. He has not commanded an army in battle. He
has only fourteen hand-picked companions with him
when he arrives at Heorot. Beowulf is best known for
the strength of his grip. This is something that would be
essential for a wrestler but not particularly useful for a
warrior living in an age dominated by edged weapons.
The victory over the sea brutes is also odd. Like his grip
strength, Beowulf's swimming and sea-creature killing
skills are impressive but not the typical skills of a conventional war-fighter. Battling beasts is more typical for a
big game hunter than a war-fighter. Finally, although it is
not entirely clear what a troll nest is like or why someone
would raid it, trolls are an undeniably unconventional enemy. Beowulf is familiar not just with the use of a sword,
a conventional weapon of the time, but he has other skills,
such as being able to swim great distances in armor. He
has all the skills of an ancient, conventional war-fighter,
but he also has skills and experience that would aid him
in the fight against an unconventional enemy. If Grendel
is the first insurgent in English literature, then Beowulf is
the first Special Forces and counterinsurgency war-fighter.

Grendel has a strategy of selective terror by targeting the leaders of Hrothgar's kingdom who spend the night at Heorot. Beowulf makes it very clear to Hrothgar that Grendel's strategy to inspire terror has not worked with him. He is not afraid. He is not there to negotiate. His strategy is not to go looking for Grendel during the day. He does not plan on defeating Grendel with a snare or a trap, or through the use of what we might call standoff weaponry, such as a bow. He plans to spend the night in Heorot hall and, if Grendel shows up, to close on the creature and kill him. He is following one of the first rules of counterinsurgency warfare: defend the population from the predations of the insurgents.

After the Danes and Geats finish their introductions, Beowulf is determined to be a worthy man who at least has a chance of killing Grendel, a feast is held at Heorot in his honor. As it grows later in the day, the Danes abandon the hall out of fear of Grendel. Beowulf and his men bed down to get some sleep and await the arrival of the monster. When Grendel arrives, as expected, he sees the motionless Geats in the hall, all apparently asleep. He is engulfed in demonic glee in expectation of the slaughter. He does not realize that at the same time "mighty and canny, Hygelac's kinsman was keenly watching for the first move the monster would make."

"Canny?" This is not a word that comes to mind to describe any of the other war-fighters described in the poem, who all seem to prefer a frontal assault for maximum death and destruction. It is a good word to describe a resourceful and unconventional war-fighter like Beowulf. He is not asleep but, rather, simply pretending to sleep while observing and gathering information about his enemy, much like a camouflaged, motionless hunter waiting for his prey. Grendel grabs one of the Geats, tears him limb from limb, and then eats him. Beowulf does not leap up to avenge his butchered comrade. Instead, he remains motionless, focused on the mission to kill Grendel, even if it means individual Geats must die.

Beowulf realizes that Grendel's strategy of night attacks on the sleepers in Heorot is predictable. The Geat is able to use this information to develop his own counterstrategy. When Grendel leans over Beowulf in the same, routine way he has leaned over so many men in the past before he killed them, he does not realize that the man lying below him, apparently fast asleep and defenseless, was actually waiting for him to come within reach of his secret weapon- an unbreakable grip. Grendel has walked into a trap:

> The captain of evil discovered himself in a handgrip harder than anything he had ever encountered in any man on the face of the earth. Every bone on his body quailed and recoiled, but he could not escape. He was desperate to flee to his den and hide with the devils litter, for in all his days he had never been clamped or cornered like this…the dread of the land was desperate to escape, to take a roundabout road and flee to his lair in the fens…. And now the timbers trembled and sang… the two contenders crashed through the building. The hall clattered and hammered, but somehow survived the onslaught and kept standing… then an extraordinary wail arose, and a bewildering fear came over the Danes. Everyone felt

it who heard that cry as it echoed off the wall, a
God-cursed scream and strain of catastrophe, the
howl of the loser, the lament of the hell-serf keen-
ing his wound. [lxxvi]

The predator Grendel is now the prey of Beowulf. The
monster is unable to break Beowulf's grip, his arm is literally ripped out of the socket as he struggles to escape. He
flees the hall but leaves his arm and a blood trail so heavy
that it leaves no doubt that he has been fatally wounded.

The Danes' and Geats' joy after the defeat of Grendel is
cut short by Grendel's mother's visit to Heorot. Hrothgar
is completely distraught after this attack by a new enemy
of the Clan of Cain that results in the death of Aeschere:

Sorrow has returned. Alas for the Danes! Aeschere
is dead. He was... a soul-mate to me, a true men-
tor, my right hand man when the ranks clashed
and our boar-crests had to take a battering in the
line of action. Aeschere was everything the world
admires in a wise man and a friend. [lxxvii]

It is only now that Hrothgar mentions to Beowulf that
more than one Grendel- like creature has been sighted
in his kingdom. He then describes a swampy area the
Danes believe to be the home of Grendel and his mother.
Beowulf responds to Hrothgar that now is not the time
for mourning and that the best thing to do is to be relentless and hunt down and kill Grendel's kin. After listening
to Beowulf, Hrothgar is able to collect himself. Beowulf
and some of his men, chosen because they are "good judg-
es of the lie of the land," track Grendel's mother to her

lair. The ability to follow or conceal tracks is not required by Hrothgar's conventional war-fighters, but it is essential for hunters or Special Forces, like our modern-day Seal Air Land Forces (SEALs), who typically operate in small groups, not unlike Beowulf and his companions.

Beowulf once again displays his skill as an unconventional war-fighter in the battle with the dragon. He studies his enemy and adopts unorthodox equipment—the iron shield—before engaging his enemy. He also gathers intelligence from one person who knows where the dragon's lair is, the slave who stole the cup in the first place. Beowulf has the skill and knowledge of conventional and unconventional warfare to defend the Geats from their enemies. He is not just a war-fighter, but also a just king who understands and cares about his people, and under his rule Geat society thrives. The last lines of the poem describe him as "the man most gracious and fair-minded, kindest to his people." [lxxviii]

Beowulf is a hero, but he is not perfect. His desire to win personal fame influences his decision to fight the dragon alone, even though the monster has been devastating the lands and lives of all the Geats. Beowulf is mistaken when he says the battle with the dragon is his fight and his fight alone; every Geat has a stake in defeating the dragon. The bond of allegiance that exists between the young Beowulf and the Geats who accompanied him to Heorot to fight Grendel is not as strong as the ones the thanes feel for King Beowulf many years later when he faces the dragon. In the battle against Grendel the men would not leave their leader to fight alone; instead they spent the night with him in the hall and tried to help him, however ineffectively, with their bladed weapons. In the battle against Grendel's mother they followed Beowulf as far as they could, right up to the water's edge. They waited there faithfully until Beowulf returned to them. This spirit of unity of purpose that is so evident in the earlier battles against Grendel and Grendel's mother is scarce in the battle with the dragon. It is manifested only when Wiglaf and Beowulf crouch together behind the iron shield and with their combined strength are able to kill the dragon.

Beowulf's pursuit of honor, fame, and glory lead him to decide to face the dragon alone. He fails to realize the need for a team effort to defend the Geat community against a deadly enemy. Beowulf seems to have forgotten Hrothgar's warning about the dangers of pride, and there may have been some truth to Unferth's accusations that Beowulf is willing to take unnecessary risks for his own personal glory. The pursuit of honor by an individual and the bonding of individuals together to achieve a common goal can act in synergy, complementing one another, so that each war-fighter endeavors to excel in combat as part of his/her role of defending the community against enemies while the community strives to support the individual war-fighter in battle. They can also be in conflict, when the war-fighter pursues personal glory, power, and wealth, to the detriment of the community. It is also possible for members of a community to support one another slavishly and unthinkingly, without questioning if their actions are truly honorable. The tension between individual pursuit of honor, fame, fortune, and glory and the needs of the community was a fundamental problem for ancient Anglo-Saxon society, and it is a problem for us today. It is never perfectly resolved in the poem, and this is part of the tragic vision of *Beowulf*. In order for us to understand the potential constructive synergy and avoid the danger of conflict between the individual's pursuit of honor and the needs of the community, we must study this tragic vision.

CHAPTER 5
Fate: The Tragic Vision of Beowulf

Beowulf begins and ends with a funeral. Between the funerals, the poem is filled with dismemberments, decapitations, death in other manners, and lots of destruction. Hrothgar's construction of Heorot Hall and the civil society around it provokes Grendel's campaign of terror against the Danes. As a result, Hrothgar's life is transformed from one of wealth and privilege into one filled with pain and suffering. He is "humiliated...numb with grief but... no respite."[lxxix]

Grendel is also a tragic figure. He lives in a cave under a lake with his mother. He "dwelt for a time in misery among the banished monsters... harrowed [tormented]... to hear the din of the loud banquet hall." [lxxx] He suffers a horrible, painful death, literally at the hands of Beowulf. Grendel's mother is stricken by grief when her son is killed, and she herself is killed soon thereafter. The poet reveals Heorot Hall itself will eventually be destroyed, in spite of Beowulf's heroic victory over Grendel, in "a barbarous burning." [lxxxi]

Beowulf's kingdom is attacked by a dragon. All but one of his comrades abandons him when he fights the creature. The dragon kills him. The dragon is the victim of the theft of a golden cup from his treasure hoard. The hoard itself is the remnant of the wealth of an ancient tribe that once thrived but has died off. The thief of the cup is a terrified servant of a cruel master. After Beowulf dies, we learned of a terrified Geat woman:

> Sang out in grief; with hair bound up, she un-burdened herself of her worst fears, a wild litany of nightmare and lament: her nation invaded, enemies on the rampage, bodies in piles, slavery in abasement...[lxxxii]

The poem has a profoundly pessimistic view of the human condition. There are occasional happy moments in the poem, like when the Danes celebrate Beowulf's victories, or when the Geats welcome Beowulf home, and there are many good and admirable people in the poem—like Hrothgar, Beowulf, and Wiglaf—but the characters in *Beowulf* exist in a world where tragedy is taken for granted. The poem is filled with reminders of the transient nature of human existence and the futility of human efforts against the ravages of time and forces of chaos.

Virtually every civilization throughout history had had a tragic vision of the world. According to the ancient Norse mythology of Scandinavia, our world is ruled by gods who live in an inaccessible place called Asgard. The Norse legends tell many stories about the adventures of the gods as they fight to defend the world against the forces of destruction and chaos, which are personified in the form of enemy giants. The powerful Norse gods are led by Odin, who is a "wild and amazing figure, by no means reliable... the fickle god who [has] his favorites but [does] not keep them forever... [he was] openly regarded as one whose oath could not be trusted." He is the "Valfather," or the father of the slain.

His servants, the Valkyries, constantly roam the earth, gathering up the brave warriors killed in battle and bringing them to Valhalla, the "slain hall." There they wait until the end of time, when the gods and these chosen warriors will fight against the giants in Ragnarok, a battle they know they are destined to lose and that will result in the destruction of the worlds of gods and men. [lxxxiii] The knowledge of their fate does not prevent them from enjoying their lives or fighting valiantly to defend this world, but they do not expect to win or break even, to be rewarded for their efforts, or for there to be a happy ending.

The pagan Anglo-Saxons who first heard the poem also seemed to have had a very pessimistic view of the world. Much of what we know about them is through the writings of Christians, and we only have fragmented records of their beliefs. Bede's *Ecclesiastical History of the English People,* which was written in 731 A.D., around the time of the Christian conversion of England, records a story allegedly told by a pagan Anglo-Saxon counselor to his chief after listening to the arguments of a Christian missionary who was trying to convert them:

> This is how the present life of man on earth, king, appears to me in comparison with that time which is unknown to us. You are sitting feasting with your ealdormen and thegns in winter time; the fire is burning on the hearth in the middle of the hall and all inside is warm, while outside the wintry storms of rain and snow are raging; and a

sparrow flies swiftly through the hall. It enters in at one door and quickly flies out the other. For the few moments it is inside, the storm of the wintry tempest cannot touch it, but after the briefest moment of calm, it flits from your sight, out of the wintry storm and into it again. So this life of man appears but for a moment; what follows or indeed what went before, we know not at all. If this new doctrine brings us more certain information, it seems right that we should accept it. [lxxxiv]

Bede also tells a story about an Italian missionary who traveled to northern England to convert the Northumbrian King Edwin. The king arranges a conference so that he and all of his priests and counselors can hear about the Christian religion and, if they are persuaded, then convert to the new religion. According to the Bede, a priest named Coifi says:

I frankly admit that, for my part, I have found that the religion which we have hitherto held has no virtue or profit to it. None of your followers has devoted himself more earnestly than I have to the worship of our gods, but nevertheless there are many who receive greater benefits and greater honor from you than I do and are more successful in their undertaking. If the gods had any power they would have helped me more readily, seeing that I have always served them with greater zeal. So it follows that if, on examination, these new doctrines which have been explained to us are found to be any better or more effectual, let us accept them at once without delay. [lxxxv]

At least according to Bede, the Anglo-Saxons had a fatalistic outlook on the world.

The Scandinavians and the Anglo-Saxons were by no means the only civilizations with a tragic vision of the human condition. In his book *Achilles in Vietnam: Combat Trauma and the Undoing of Character,* Jonathan Shay, MD. Ph. D. discusses the tragic vision of the ancient Greeks. He writes that in their culture it was possible to "speak of the gods as cruel, crooked, or heartless," and that the warriors of ancient Greece "did not expect the gods to be other than what they were: powerful, self-centered, arbitrary, unpredictable, heartless and cruel." [lxxxvi] As a result, there was no expectation among the ancient Greeks that life was supposed to be happy, fair, or just.

Shay gives an example of this tragic vision of the human condition in Homer's epic poem *The Iliad,* the chronicle of the war between the ancient Greeks and Trojans. Helen, the wife of the Greek king Menelaus, leaves her husband to live with Paris, son of Priam, the king of Troy. The Greeks are enraged by this dishonor done to their leader and decide to wage war on the Trojans. The Greeks and Trojans begin to fight, but the death and destruction soon make everyone wish for a swift end to the war. Both sides agree to settle the conflict by single combat between Menelaus and Paris. If Menelaus is killed, then the Greeks sail home, leaving Helen and treasure behind with the Trojans. If Paris dies, the Trojans return Helen to the Greeks and pay annual tribute to Greece.

When word spreads of the combat "all hearts lift-
ed—for both sides hoped for an end of miserable war,"
Menelaus and Paris meet each other on the plains of Troy.
Paris is no match for Menelaus, and his death and the
end of the conflict seems imminent. However, the human desire for an end to the fighting is thwarted by the
goddess Aphrodite, who wraps Paris up in a cloud and
transports him off the battlefield before Menelaus kills
him. As a result, the war drags on, resulting in the deaths
of innumerable Greeks and Trojans, and the eventual sack
of Troy. [lxxxvii]

The Judeo-Christian worldview has a transcendent
faith in a just and loving God who will lead the faithful
to paradise in the afterlife. However, it has a tragic vision of the human condition here on Earth. In the Old
Testament Adam and Eve are expelled from Eden because they disobey God and eat the fruit of the tree of
knowledge of good and evil. God specifically tells Adam
in Genesis 3:17-19 that as a result of his disobedience he
will struggle:

> Cursed is the ground because of you; through
> painful toil you will eat of it all the days of your
> life. It will produce thorns and thistles for you,
> and you will eat the plants of the field. By the
> sweat of your brow you will eat your food un-
> til you return to the ground since from it you
> were taken; for dust you are and to dust you will
> return... [lxxxviii]

The story of Cain and Abel, as discussed earlier, shows
just how dysfunctional the earliest family was. The Old

Testament contains chapter after chapter filled with verse after verse describing savage warfare between the Isrealites and the Amalekites, Amorites, and many other tribes, as well as the violent rise and fall of the Hittite, Assyrian, Egyptian, and other empires. The book of Job describes the story of a good man whom God allows Satan to torture for no apparent reason. Job describes his situation:

> Does not man have hard service on earth? Are not his days like those of a hired man? Like a slave longing for the evening shadows, or a hired man waiting eagerly for his wages, so I have been allotted months of futility, and nights of misery have been assigned to me. When I lie down I think, 'How long before I get up?' The night drags on, and I toss till dawn. My body is clothed with worms and scabs. My skin is broken and festering... Why have you made me your target? [lxxxix]

Job puts into words the Old Testament's tragic vision of what life can be like on Earth.

The New Testament continues along a similar theme. It is filled with persecutions and injustices perpetrated upon undeserving victims. Jesus Christ Himself is crucified, and almost all of His apostles are killed in gruesome ways for their faith. St. Augustine was one of the great Christian thinkers of the classical age. His writings present a vision of human beings as being so mired in sin, so full of false pride, and so egocentric that they can never establish a truly just and fair society here on Earth because they will always eventually succumb to pursuing their own personal advantages or pleasures, even if it hurts the people around them. [xc] He and other Christian thinkers command believers to imitate their savior, Jesus Christ, and cheerfully take up their burdens and sufferings, as Christ did the cross, with the full knowledge that they may be persecuted here on Earth for their faith.

America's founding fathers were profoundly influenced by the Judeo-Christian and classical vision of human nature as flawed and corrupt. As a result, when they wrote the Constitution they intentionally divided the powers of the state among many different government offices and departments in order to prevent any one individual or small group from consolidating power over the American people, arguing that "if men were angels, no government would be necessary." [xci]

The idea that life can and should be fair, easy, and pleasant is a rare one in human civilizations. It has gained prominence in the West, beginning with the Enlightenment of the 1700s. It was promulgated by writers like Godwin in England, Diderot and Voltaire in France. They had faith in the essential goodness of man, in spite of the evidence of history. They also believed in the power of human reason, and that with education the human race would inevitably progress to a higher state of perfections. [xcii] This is what gives modern culture "its optimistic treatment of the problem of evil." [xciii] It has led to the creation of America's current generation of leaders who

> have by and large been men and women who had fortunate lives, who always seemed to expect nice things to happen and happiness to occur....

They claimed to be quintessentially optimistic but it was a cheap optimism, based more on sunny personal experience than any particular faith, and void of any understanding of how dark and gritty life can be, and has been for most of human history. [xciv]

As a result, it is virtually impossible for America's elites, typically products of affluent, secular backgrounds and steeped in Enlightenment thinking, to grasp why there is war at all, since according to their worldview human beings are fundamentally rational, moral creatures, and no reasonable person would ever participate in anything as irrational, destructive, and tragic as war. This utopian vision of human nature and irrational faith in human reason, which flies in the face of human history, separates them from previous generations. It makes it difficult, if not impossible, for most of them to conceive that someone or something could have an inexplicable, unexplainable, illogical "hard grudge" that drives that person to kill. They do not grasp that conflict and war have been the norm and that peace has been the exception in human existence, something was well understood by ancient Greek warriors, medieval Vikings, Anglo-Saxons, and just about everyone else in the world throughout history.

The debate in America about the war in Iraq is in part a symptom of this dysfunctional utopian vision. It was hard to have sympathy for Saddam Hussein. He:

was not a man of the people or a friend of the Arab people. The fact is, Saddam Hussein killed more Arabs than anyone in the history of mankind. There was nothing he wouldn't do to secure his grip on the country, and there were no principles he would not sacrifice for the sake of his own power and greed. [xcv]

Saddam was not an enlightened, good-natured, rational man amenable to resolving disputes through discussion. He was a vicious killer. During his rule he invaded Iran, Kuwait, and slaughtered thousands of Kurdish and Shiite Iraqis. His relentless pursuit of wealth and power is incomprehensible to an Enlightenment-minded thinker, but the marauding Vikings, medieval Anglo-Saxons, and the ancient Hittites and Assyrians would have understood him perfectly.

After the attack on the Twin Towers in 2001, President George W. Bush argued that Saddam was trying to obtain weapons of mass destruction, and at least prior to 2003 the majority of members of the U.S. Congress supported the war against Saddam, in part because they agreed with President Bush about the Iraqi dictator's intentions. [xcvi] Furthermore, based on the evidence available at the time, many thought that Saddam might have been planning to give the weapons of mass destruction to terrorists to use in an attack on America or another country, and that this might have caused death and destruction several orders of magnitude larger than what resulted from the attack on the Twin Towers in New York on September 11, 2001. On the other hand, Saddam might not have been trying to get weapons of mass destruction. Or, he might have been trying to make people think he was trying to get weapons of mass destruction as part of a bluff to deter and intimidate his enemies. We will never know for sure.

As a result of weighing a lot of mights, maybes, and what-ifs colored by personal opinions, the Bush administration decided to lead a coalition of nations in an invasion against Saddam Hussein in 2003. This led to the tragic death of thousands of Iraqis and Coalition forces. There was a breakdown of law and order in Iraq after Saddam was overthrown, resulting in more death and destruction. The power vacuum created an environment that allowed Al-Qaeda to flourish, resulting in even more tragic deaths of Iraqis and Coalition forces. However, it is possible that the invasion of Iraq and the overthrow of Saddam prevented him from murdering untold more millions of people. After Saddam, things could have gone from bad to worse if his cruel and sadistic sons, Uday and Qusay, continued the brutal dynasty. We just don't know what might have happened if he had not been deposed.

The Bush administration made mistakes. This is not unique or an aberration in human history. It is just another manifestation of the tragic condition humans find themselves in as they muddle through life. The question is not whether there were bad things that happened as a result of the invasion of Iraq. There were. The situation in Iraq was tragic, and the question before the invasion of 2003 was which course of action was the least horrible, then how to best pursue it.

In *Beowulf* the hero defeats Grendel; he defeats warfighters from rival tribes; and finally, he defeats a dragon. He also dies and leaves his people kingless and vulnerable to the predations of neighboring tribes. He is not perfect, and his decisions have both good and tragic consequences. In this respect, he is not so unlike the leaders of our time. If we do not appreciate the tragic nature of the human condition that underlies the worldview in *Beowulf*, we will be doomed to stumble from one world crisis or conflict to the next, continually surprised that events in the real world are not always fair and often have unhappy endings.

Fortunately, *Beowulf* is not just about death, destruction, and funerals. It also offers hope concerning how human beings can overcome and transcend their transient, tragic condition through the pursuit of honor and through dedicating themselves to the welfare of others— that is, by practicing the virtue that Tacitus, the Roman observer of the ancient Germans, called *comitatus*. The virtues of honor and *comitatus* guided the Anglo-Saxons as they fought their way through life, and they can help guide us through the tragic conflicts of the modern age.

CHAPTER 6
The Honorable War-Fighter: No Better Friend, No Worse Enemy

Honor: Beowulf is obsessed with it. His pursuit of it through heroic deeds is one of the central themes of the poem. Honor is a word we don't use too much nowadays, and when we do it is usually in an ironic or even sarcastic manner. However, the concept is still with us: even if we use different words, like prestige, integrity, or success to describe it, people still strive for it.

Before the fight with Grendel, Beowulf is an obscure thane of Hygalec. His hunger for honor and fame is one of the forces driving him to seek out and fight the creature. When Beowulf arrives at Hrothgar's court, Unferth questions his honor, or what we might term his credibility, as a war-fighter and his qualifications to fight Grendel by relating the story of how Beowulf was defeated by his friend Breca in a frivolous, foolish swimming contest where both he and his family nearly drowned. Beowulf responds by explaining that he could have beaten Breca, but instead he did the truly honorable thing by killing the sea monsters that infested the waters and threatened the lives of sailors, even if it meant losing the contest.

Beowulf is forthright and honorable when he tells Hrothgar and his court exactly why he left the land of the Geats and traveled to the land of the Danes:

I had a fixed purpose when I put to sea. As I sat in the boat with my band of men, I meant to perform to the utmost what your people wanted or perish in the attempt in the fiend's clutches. And I shall fulfill that purpose, prove myself with a proud deed or meet my death here in the mead hall. xcvii

Such boasts about killing or being killed in combat are common in the pages of heroic literature. What is unusual is the way Beowulf chooses to fight Grendel:

When it comes to fighting, I count myself as dangerous any day as Grendel. So it won't be a cutting edge I'll wield to mow him down, easily as I might. He has no idea of the arts of war, of shield or sword-play, although he does possess a wild strength. No weapons, therefore, for either this night: unarmed he shall face me if face me he dares. xcviii

This is a remarkable thing for Beowulf to say. Grendel has never shown any sign of honor or mercy in his campaign of terror against the Danes, and Beowulf does not know that Grendel cannot be injured by bladed weapons, yet the Geat war-fighter still decides to eschew any edged weapons because he believes this will make the fight a fair and equal one.

Beowulf is as good as his word and defeats Grendel in hand-to-hand combat. He is respectful to Grendel while the creature is alive, but then, after the terrible battle, Beowulf is disrespectful to Grendel and his entire clan when he displays the mangled arm that he ripped from the body of Grendel "high up near the roof" of Heorot Hall. [xcix] Grendel is a formidable opponent who has single-handedly fought Hrothgar and his entire army for twelve long years. His strength and ferocity in battle have not won him any friends among the Danes, but they respect his skills as a war-fighter. Beowulf's use of Grendel's arm as a gory trophy for public display is a dishonorable desecration of Grendel's body. It is an action that helps to provoke Grendel's grieving mother to revenge. She goes to the hall to kill those who killed her son and to recover the arm in spite of the danger she faces from the Danish warriors in the hall. The poem never explores the possibility that perhaps Grendel's mother would have never attacked the Danes if the body of her son had been treated with respect and honor.

Other cultures, like the ancient Greeks, were also obsessed with honor. The advice a father gives to his son in *the Iliad* is to "always be the best, my boy, the bravest, and hold your head above the others." [c] The concept of respect toward an enemy is not well-developed in Beowulf, but it is one of the central themes of *The Iliad,* where the combatants fight ferociously, but always with the expectation that both sides will honor a truce to allow for the collection of the dead from the battlefield for a proper burial. [ci] Achilles fails to treat the corpse of his Trojan opponent Hector with honor and respect: he instead drags the body behind his chariot outside the walls of Troy as a result of his uncontrollable rage and grief over the death of his friend Patrocles. [cii] This behavior is completely contrary to the advice to "always be the best," and Achilles' behavior is considered a disgraceful act of disrespect by Greeks and

Trojans alike. The desecration of the dead in both *Beowulf* and *The Iliad* serves to inflame passions that result in more death and destruction.

Different cultures have different perceptions of what constitutes dishonorable behavior. In feudal Japan it was not uncommon for samurai to decapitate their opponent's heads, but this was not done out of disrespect but rather because they needed the heads to show to their superiors in order to be rewarded for their services, i.e. get paid. In fact, there is a story about a samurai named Kimurai Shinegari, who perfumed his head in order to make it a more pleasant trophy if it was ever taken by an opponent (which it eventually was). [ciii] There is a sort of universal golden rule for professional war-fighters to regard each other as "comrades in arms" and to treat one another with respect in both peace and war. Through the act of showing respect for an enemy, an individual validates their own worthiness because if the enemy is formidable, then they themselves must be a formidable war-fighter to challenge such an enemy, and they themselves must also be worthy of respect. This validates their self-respect and maintains their sense of honor. [civ] This concept is articulated in our own time by the U.S. Marines, who describe themselves as "no better friend and no worse enemy." If, in contrast, an enemy is viewed as being dishonorable and unworthy of respect, then it is only a small step toward committing atrocities against them. When combatants commit atrocities in an effort to celebrate their victories or terrorize their opponent, their actions are usually met with reciprocal acts of violence by their enraged and antagonized enemies. The result is a spiral of increasing violence that prolongs and intensifies the conflict.

Some of the most dramatic examples of this phenomenon happened not distant ages ago, when *Beowulf* was written, but in our own time. In World War II the Nazi ideology taught the German soldier fighting on the Eastern Front that he was part of a "quasi-religious, anti-Bolshevik, and racial crusade" and that his opponents were *Untermenschen* who were inferior to the German people, personal enemies of Hitler and of the German people. Colonel-General Hermann Hoth, a German officer on the Eastern Front, told his men:

> Here in the East spiritually unbridgeable conceptions are fighting each other: German sense of honor and race, and a soldierly tradition of many centuries, against an Asiatic mode of thinking and primitive instincts, whipped up by a small number of mostly Jewish intellectuals: fear of the knout, disregard of moral values, leveling down, throwing away of one's worthless life. More than ever we are filled with the thought of a new era, in which the strength of the German people's racial superiority and achievements entrust it with the leadership of Europe. We clearly recognize our mission to save European culture from the advancing Asiatic barbarism. We now know that we have to fight against an incensed and tough opponent. This battle can only end with the destruction of one or the other; a compromise is out of the question.[cv]

As a result of this attitude, German soldiers did not hesitate to loot Russian towns and villages or to murder

Russian prisoners of war or civilians. The atrocities helped provoke fanaticism in Communist troops resulting in the torturing and killing of captured German soldiers, mutilating the bodies of dead Germans, and other atrocities that resulted in a cycle of German and Russian atrocities and reprisals.

One former German non-commissioned officer who fought on the Eastern front was interviewed almost forty years after the war. He told the story of how his unit was ambushed by the Soviets and forced to withdraw. When they returned the next day to recover the bodies of their comrades, they found that the bodies had been mutilated, with eyes, "gouged out. Genitals cut off." He went on to admit that the Germans had done similar things to dead Soviet soldiers. He concluded, "It was really like that, what you do to me, I do to you." [cvi] The Nazi ideology's dehumanization of the Soviet enemy and the Communist ideology's dehumanization of the German soldier were major factors contributing to the savage of war of annihilation and extermination between Nazi Germany and the Soviet Union in World War II. The striking exception to the brutality and atrocities committed by Nazi Germany is Field Marshall Erwin Rommel:

> Belonged heart and soul to the professional tradition of the German Army, where... [the] medieval ideal of knighthood (Ritterlichkeit) persisted in little-impaired form until the advent of Hitler. Noted for his correct treatment of prisoners... In his professional opponents, he inspired admiration and awe... [cvii]

His sense of honor led to restraint on the battlefield, but it did not diminish his effectiveness as a war-fighter and leader. He gradually lost faith in the German war effort and became disillusioned with the Nazi party as he learned more about it and the atrocities committed under its rule. Hitler learned of this and forced Rommel to commit suicide in 1944.

The war on the Eastern Front between Nazi Germany and the Soviet Union was not the only place where combatants regarded their opponents as being less than honorable, inferior human beings, thereby creating an environment that facilitated cruelty and barbarism. In the Pacific theater during World War Two, the Japanese and the Americans viewed each other as mentally, physically, and morally inferior, unworthy of respect. The Imperial Japanese leadership promulgated myths about the Japanese people as being members of the "Yamamoto race." The Japanese people were even told that they were descendants from gods, that they were not just genetically but also morally purer than other people, and that they were the "sole superior race in the world." [cviii] The Greater East Asia Prosperity sphere that Japan planned to establish after driving the European powers out of Asia would be run by members of a superior race—namely themselves. [cix]

This ideology of Japanese superiority to European, Chinese, Filipino and other ethnic groups contributed to the atrocities like the Rape of Nanking and the Bataan death march, in which thousands of prisoners of war as well as civilians were shot, bayoneted, beheaded, or drowned for no tactical, operational, or strategic military purpose. This savagery only galvanized opposition to Japanese imperialism and increased resistance to the invading Japanese forces.

At the same time that the Japanese were being told they were superior to their enemies, Americans were being told that they were superior to the Japanese, who were said to be primitive, immature, emotionally unstable, and collectively inclined to violence. At the beginning of the war, U.S. troops were told that their opponents suffered from severe physical defects in their inner ear balance systems, as well as myopia, and as a result could not fly planes. Both Japan and America created a stereotype of the enemy as being inferior and unworthy of being treated with respect and honor. J. Glenn Gray, a World war two combat veteran, describes the results:

> The ugliness of war against any enemy conceived to be subhuman can hardly be exaggerated... Yet this image of the enemy as beast lessens even the satisfaction of destruction, for there is not proper regard for the worth of the objects destroyed. [cx]

The end results on both sides were "arrogance, viciousness, atrocity and death." [cxi]

The story of Vietnam was a similar one. American soldiers were told that their enemy was

> Primitive, ignorant, superstitious, and not rational... In Vietnam, when Americans witnessed the determination and self-sacrifice of enemy soldiers, they were taught that enemy soldiers placed no value on their own lives. They were called madmen and animals and said to lack any emotions.

In addition to being dirty and smelling bad, the
enemy was puny and ugly. [cxii]

This disrespect and dehumanization of the enemy in
Vietnam had disastrous results for America. First and
foremost, it led Americans to underestimate their opponent. The guerilla tactics of the Viet Cong were seen as
"cowardly," the acts of men and women who were not
"real soldiers," [cxiii]when in fact they were extremely effective and led to ultimate victory for the North Vietnamese.
Death and defeat on the battlefield were not the only
tragedies that resulted from the Vietnam War. The deper-
sonalization, dehumanization, and dishonorable regard
for the enemy in Vietnam contributed to some American
Vietnam War veterans' feelings of alienation, emotional
numbness, and an inability to experience pleasure. [cxiv]
Jonathan P. Shay, a psychiatrist who has worked with
Vietnam veterans for decades, concludes, "the impulse to
dehumanize and disrespect the enemy must be resisted,
whether its basis is religious, nationalistic, or racist. The
soldier's physical and psychological survival is at stake." [cxv]
Beowulf shows honor when he declines to use edged
weapons against Grendel. In Homer's *Iliad* the war-fighters on both the Greek and Trojan side regard each other
as worthy opponents, deserving of respect and honor.
[cxvi] but, does literature imitate real life in this case? Can
America successfully defend itself against enemies who do
not honor or respect us and do not hesitate to employ terror and brutality in order to win?
The answer is yes. In 2003, U.S. and coalition forces
waged one of the greatest *blitzkrieg* campaigns in history against Saddam Hussein and his Baathist regime.

It took US forces only a few months to crush Saddam's conventional forces. By late April 2003, most of the fighting between conventional forces was over. Many Baath party officials were forbidden to participate in the formation of the new Iraqi government. Unfortunately, the vast majority of the administrators, as well as the civilian and military leaders, were members of the Baath party. This did not necessarily mean they were ardent supporters of Saddam: it was simply something people had been forced to do in order to get a decent job under Saddam's totalitarian regime. The American and coalition forces had inadvertently treated these Iraqis in a disrespectful and dishonorable manner, prejudging them to be ardent supporters of Saddam's brutal regime when, in fact, most of them were just trying to get along and take care of themselves and their families under a brutal tyrant. Things got worse when the US and Coalition forces decided to disband the Iraqi army, many of whom were professional soldiers with minimal if any interest in politics. In *The Strongest Tribe*, Bing West writes that the night after the decision to dissolve the Iraqi army was announced, USMC Major General "Mad Dog" Mattis was asked by one of his lieutenants "when all those out-of-work pissed-off Iraqi soldiers… would start an insurgency." [cxvii] The answer was a few weeks, and by the summer of 2003 there was a full-scale insurgency against the U.S. and coalition forces in Iraq:

> Tribal fighters comprised most of the insurgents. Determined to drive out the infidel invaders… they say themselves as the honorable resistance. They had no overarching political goal. These

were 18-year-olds with AK-47's and no money, no prospect of marriage or sex, no music, no recreation, no job, and no direction given by elders whose status had been demeaned by invaders who didn't speak the language… [cxviii]

The insurgency grew in strength and numbers, a mixture of Baathists, Al-Qaeda, and various Sunni and Shia extremists, loosely united in their common goal of killing Americans and coalition forces. By 2007 the violence was so great that U.S. Senate Majority leader Harry Reid told the American people that the war in Iraq was lost [cxix] and that the United States had no choice but to withdraw from Iraq in defeat.

Not everyone agreed with Senator Reid. Former Secretary of State Henry Kissinger wrote an op-ed piece in the *Washington Post* in which he stared, "Victory over the insurgency… is the only meaningful exit strategy." [cxx] At around the same time, the Combined Arms Center in Leavenworth, Kansas, released *counterinsurgency Field Manual* **3-24**. The book is based on the premise that the American war-fighter is "a guest in a country where people deserved to be treated with the same respect as us at home. Shooting wildly in response to an attack or trashing a home provoked anger and a desire for revenge. If he acted as a bully, he was recruiting for the insurgents…" [cxxi] With the selection of a counter-insurgency warfare expert, General Petreus, to lead U.S. forces in Iraq, a new strategy was devised that was based on respect for the Iraqi people and their aspirations for a better life. The new tactics focused on establishing rule of law, a market economy, and some form of representative government. All of these goals are based on the assumption that the average Iraqi is someone of intelligence and integrity, worthy of honor and respect. The result was the destruction of the insurgency, a dramatic decline in violence, a dramatic growth of the Iraqi economy, and the resurgence of civil society in Iraq. All these good things are based on the realization that many Iraqis may have fought against Americans, but that does not mean that they are not honorable and worthy of American respect. The war in Iraq against Al-Qaeda was fought and won on a strategy that is founded on honor and respect, for not only America war-fighters, but also for Iraqi and other enemy war-fighters.

Beowulf's last battle against the dragon is fought in the pursuit of honor, but it leads to the death of the hero and disaster for his people. He fought Grendel to protect Heorot Hall from his predations. He fought for his king Hygalec to defend the Geat people against enemies. However, when he fights the dragon alone, it is primarily for his own personal pursuit of fame. His relentless pursuit of glory and fame preclude pursuing other options, such as returning the golden cup or having his companions accompany him into battle, sharing the glory with them and living to fight another day as king and defender of the Geats. Leaders pursuing their own agenda to increase their personal wealth, prestige, and honor, to the detriment of their people, is something all too familiar to modern Americans. One of the most dramatic examples is the failure of American leadership in the Vietnam War.

After the end of the Second World War, the European empires that had existed for centuries collapsed within a few years. The Vietnamese drove their French rulers out of their country in the 1950. [cxxii] The United States was concerned that this would create a power vacuum that would allow Communist forces to expand into Indochina, and so during the 1960's the U.S. gradually began committing more and more forces to the defense of South Vietnam against the Communist North Vietnamese. President Lyndon Baines Johnson chose William McNamara as his secretary of defense to lead the war effort against the North Vietnamese. McNamara had worked in the business sector but had no military experience. He was a strong-willed, brilliant man. He and his subordinates, known as the "whiz kids," were described as "like-minded men who shared their leader's penchant for quantitative analysis and suspicion of proposals based solely on 'military experience.' [cxxiii] They often ignored military advice in favor of advice from civilians.[cxxiv] Air Force Chief of Staff Curtis Lemay described McNamara and the "whiz kids" in more colorful terms:

> The most egotistical people that I ever saw in my life. They had no faith in the military; they had no respect for the military at all. They felt that the Harvard Business School method of solving problems would solve any problem in the world... They were better than the rest of us: otherwise they wouldn't have gotten their superior education, as they saw it...[cxxv]

McNamara and his advisors developed a strategy of "graduated pressure," which was modeled after an economically based cost-benefit analysis of the effects of the U.S. war effort on the North Vietnamese economy. The plan was for the United States slowly to increase its military presence in an effort to communicate to the North Vietnamese that continued military aggression on their part would result in increasing destruction of Vietnamese infrastructure and increasing loss of Vietnamese life. McNamara believed this rational strategy would persuade to the North Vietnamese to make a calculated decision not to remain in the business of waging war on South Vietnamese.

The North Vietnamese, who had been raised in a culture that had resisted Chinese imperial ambitions over many centuries, and many of whom had personally fought against the Imperial Japanese army in World War II and the French forces in the 1950's, correctly interpreted the strategy of graduated pressure as an indication of a lack of will and determination on the part of American political leadership to fight and win in Vietnam. H.R. McMaster, in his book *Dereliction of Duty*, writes that the strategy was fundamentally flawed, and not just because it relied heavily on bombing of fixed targets, which had little effect on an agricultural country like North Vietnam or on mobile guerrilla forces like the Viet Cong:

> Graduated pressure was fundamentally flawed in other ways. The strategy ignored the uncertainty of war and the unpredictable psychology of an activity that involves killing, death, and destruction. To the North Vietnamese, military action, involving as it did attacks on their forces and bombing of their territory, was not simply a means of communication. Human sacrifices in war evoke strong emotions, creating a dynamic that defies systems analysis quantification... The... course

of events depended not only on decisions made in Washington but also on enemy responses that were unpredictable: McNamara, however, viewed the war as another business management problem that, he assumed would ultimately succumb to his reasoned judgment and the other's rational calculations. Others expressed doubts about the utility of attacking North Vietnam by air to win a conflict in South Vietnam. Nevertheless, McNamara refused to consider the consequences of his recommendations and forged ahead oblivious of the human and psychological consequences of war...[cxxvi]

McNamara's hubris in thinking that his experiences in the business world prepared him to fight a war contributed to the tragedy of Vietnam. By 1965 the U.S. military Joint Chiefs of Staff realized the strategy of graduated pressure was a failure and that the war in Vietnam was not going well; it would require far more ground forces to win than the numbers the administration was telling the American people. However, all of them, with the exception of the Commandant of the Marine Corps, failed to speak up. Instead, they took the easy route and withheld this information from Congress. McMaster concludes that

The disaster in Vietnam was not the result of impersonal forces but a uniquely human failure, the responsibility for which was shared by President Johnson and his principal military and civilian advisors. The failures were many and reinforcing: arrogance, weakness, lying in the pursuit of self-interest, and above all, abdication of responsibility to the American people. [cxxvii]

Honor is as important in our daily lives as it was to the Anglo-Saxons who wrote down the story *Beowulf*. The breakdown of honor in American leadership during the Vietnam War was one of the central reasons why America was defeated. The pursuit of notoriety, fame, and short-term gain without regard for the consequences of one's actions can be confused with honor—at least, at first—but it eventually leads to disaster. The true pursuit of personal honor is tempered by consideration of the effects of one's behavior on the lives of the people around oneself. If the action results in harm to the community, then it is probably not entirely honorable.

The concept of *comitatus,* or commitment to the defense and service of others is another central theme of *Beowulf.* It provides the context to help determine which actions are honorable and which are foolish or destructive and it serves as a restraint to help prevent the perversion of the pursuit of honor into hubris and the reckless, unbridled, selfish pursuit of personal glory.

CHAPTER 7
Comitatus: Resilience and Cohesion Under Stress

Comitatus is the term the ancient Roman author Tacitus coined to describe the relationship between the ancient chieftains of northern Europe and the war-fighters who served them. Under the code of *comitatus*, a Germanic war-fighter would swear vows of absolute loyalty to his lord, promising to fight and, if necessary, to die for him. In return, the liege lord would give the man material support, as well as weapons, land, and status. Tacitus wrote that under the code of *comitatus*:

> it is disgraceful for the companions not to equal their chief; but it is reproach and infamy during a whole succeeding life to retreat from the field surviving him. To aid, to protect him; to place their own gallant actions to the account of his glory, is their first and most sacred engagement. The chiefs fight for glory; the companions for their chief... The companion requires from the liberality of his chief, the warlike steed, the bloody and conquering spear; and in place of pay, he expects to be supplied with a table, homely indeed, but plentiful...[cxxviii]

This code of loyalty was one of foundations of Germanic society. Tacitus also wrote that the penalty for treason, desertion, cowardice and similar breaches of this code was death. cxxix

The principal of *comitatus* guides the words and actions of the characters throughout the poem. When Beowulf and his fourteen companions arrive on the beach of Hrothgar's kingdom they are met by a sentry, who studies them closely and concludes that they are "a troop loyal to [Hrothgar].cxxx The sentry is correct in his assessment. Beowulf is there at least in part to "follow up on an old friendship" and repay Hrothgar for the favor he did for Ecgtheow, Beowulf's father, years ago, thereby fulfilling an obligation consistent with the the code of loyalty embodied by *comitatus*. cxxxi

After Beowulf and Hrothgar have been formally introduced and settle down for a feast, the old king laments that he is unable to fulfill his obligations to his men under *comitatus* and lead them to victory against Grendel. That night, when Beowulf and Grendel have their terrible battle in the hall, the Geats do no run but instead do their best to help Beowulf, even though Grendel is impervious to their weapons. When Beowulf descends beneath the surface in pursuit of Grendel's mother, he is gone for hours. Hrothgar and his men wait by the waterside, but then lose hope and leave after several hours. Beowulf's fellow Geats refuse to give up hope and do not leave the water's edge.cxxxii Their faithfulness is yet another demonstration of *comitatus*.

When Beowulf returns home, he immediately reports to his king, Hygelac. He tells of his victory over Grendel and Grendel's mother. He also gives some of Hrothgar's gifts to his king, again demonstrating *comitatus* in his allegiance to Hygalec. The king then reciprocates by rewarding Beowulf with land and cattle. Beowulf faithfully serves Hygalec for many years in peace and war. After Hygalec dies, he serves Hygalec's son faithfully, until he too dies and there is no heir, and Beowulf becomes king of the Geats. The social relations described throughout much of the poem are based on the code of *comitatus*. Beowulf rules wisely as king for 50 years. He has many thanes, who he "shared his hearth and gold with," [cxxxiii] and who in return swore to serve Beowulf in peace and war. Tragically the code of *comitatus* breaks down among the Geats in the battle against the dragon. Beowulf fails to think of what will happen to his people if he is killed by the dragon, and they are left without a king to protect and lead them. His men, who have been eating his food and accepting his gifts for many years, are all too willing to allow their king to face the dragon alone. In fact, when the battle gets hot, all the retainers except Wiglaf, a distant relative of Beowulf, run for the safety of the woods. Wiglaf articulates the code of *comitatus* when he says that he would rather be killed by dragon fire than go home after the fight alive if Beowulf is killed. He asks a rhetorical question of the other Geats: should Beowulf alone be exposed to battle? He answers his own question not with words but with deeds. He wades into the fight, and when he and Beowulf are crouched together behind Beowulf's shield and *comitatus* has been restored on a small scale between to two war-fighters, they unite to overcome the dragon.

Combat has been described as the "universal human phobia." [cxxxiv] The natural urge for most people is to run

away from it. *Njal's Saga,* which is thought to be a reason-
ably accurate portrayal of events around the tenth century
in Iceland, narrates the feud that eventually lead to the
tragic death of Njal and his sons. One of the more violent
characters described in the saga is Skarphedin Njalsson.
In one encounter, he hits an opponent with his axe "on
his head and split it down to the jaw, so the molars fell out
on the ice." On another occasion he is able to cut through
protective armor and into the shoulder of an opponent
with one swing of his axe; he then goes on to decapitate
him. On another occasion, he cuts a man's leg off at the
thigh with one swing of his axe. [cxxxv] There were good reasons to have a phobia or a fear of encountering someone
like Skarphedin Njalsson on the battlefield in the Viking
age; Vikings used weapons and tactics similar to the ones
employed by their medieval Anglo-Saxon descendants
who heard the story of *Beowulf* being told around the fire
at night, so undoubtedly some of the listeners in the origi-
nal audience had experienced the terror of encountering
someone like Skarphedin Njalsson in battle. With the
passage of time and the development of guns, poisonous
gas, Napalm, land mines, and other increasingly sophisticated weapons that kill and maim, there are now more
reasons than ever to fear combat.

Combatants are able to overcome the universal fear of
combat by creating mutual trust and support among a
group of war-fighters, or *comitatus.* The result is to trans-
form isolated individuals into an effective fighting force.
The nineteenth-century French infantry's Colonel Ardant
du Picq explained the phenomenon:

Four brave men who do not know each other will not dare to attack a lion. Four less brave men, but knowing each other well, sure of their reliability and consequently of mutual aid, will attack resolutely. [cxxxvi]

The most effective groups of war-fighters have a strong sense of *comitatus*. Military training throughout history always tries to create strong ties of discipline and comradeship among war-fighters so that

when the time comes, the troops will go on obeying their superiors' orders. At all cost, they must stay with one another and continue to fight in an organized way, even amid the chaos of battle, and even when looking death in the face. In any military worthy of the name, the entire structure is erected to support this single overriding need. [cxxxvii]

It is not easy to create this special bond of *comitatus* between individuals. In our own time, it is done through isolating recruits from the rest of society and subjecting them to vigorous physical training, close-order drill, and other intensive training programs that not only teach them the information and skills required to function as a war-fighter but also require them to band together and work as a team successfully to complete basic training. *Comitatus* is maintained among the war-fighters after they complete their initial military training through not just ongoing military exercises, but also unique uniforms, distinctive hairstyles, and social events that commemorate significant events in the history of their particular military organization. These all help maintain their sense of group identity. The distinguished history professor William H. McNeill, who served in the U.S. Army from 1941-46, wrote:

> Words… are inadequate to describe the emotion aroused by the prolonged movement in unison that drilling involved. A sense of pervasive well-being is what I recall; more specifically, a strange sense of personal enlargement; a sort of swelling out, becoming bigger than life, thanks to participation in a collective ritual. [cxxxviii]

One of the words Professor McNeill may have been looking for to describe this feeling is *comitatus*.

History is full of examples of well-disciplined, well-trained, well-led soldiers bound together by *comitatus* fighting and defeating numerically superior foes. The ancient Greek forces that fought and beat much larger Persian forces had a strong sense of *comitatus*. They employed the phalanx, a tight formation of men formed in ranks where each individual "depended on the man next to him to shield his own unprotected right side and to maintain the cohesion of the entire phalanx." [cxxxix] The better the training, the stronger the unit discipline and cohesion, the more lethal the phalanx was in battle.

Comitatus is just as relevant today as it was to the ancient Greeks, or the tribesmen of Northern Europe and Scandinavia. Nazi Forces in World War II routinely fought and defeated numerically superior opponents, in part due to superior unit cohesiveness. The German military generally formed units made of men recruited from one geographic area, which then trained together and went to war together. The German army suffered millions of casualties in the Second World War, but no combat unit ceased to be effective until physically overwhelmed by superior enemy numbers and materiel. In contrast, in World War Two Americans frequently trained with one group of individuals, then were sent to completely different units and were expected to go into combat with people who were complete strangers, resulting in decreased combat effectiveness and higher physical and psychiatric casualties. [cxl]

The stronger the spirit of *comitatus* among the warfighters within a given U.S. military unit, the better they perform in combat. In the Battle at the Chosin Reservoir during the Korean War, the U.S. Military was pinned down in the dead of winter by overwhelming numbers of advancing Communist Chinese Forces. There were Marines on the west side of the reservoir and Army units on the east side fighting to withdraw from the Communist onslaught. The two groups of American forces were isolated from one another, but they were fighting the same enemy under the same circumstances as they struggled to retreat down narrow mountain roads. The Marines had more experienced leadership and had trained and fought together longer. As a result, they were more cohesive and resilient under enemy attack and were able to withdraw with all their wounded as well as most of their vehicles and artillery, whereas the Army lost all its vehicles and equipment.

The Marines say that every marine is a rifleman and that the basic modern fighting unit is the rifle platoon. USMC General Trainor, who fought at the battle of Chosin Reservoir, wrote that a platoon is

> a flesh-and-blood organization that is in the most dangerous of businesses. There are lots of peoples and things behind that make up a war machine. But there is nothing in front of a rifle platoon but the enemy and possible death. Its members must care for one another. Its leaders must cherish the men in every fire team and squad. [cxli]

The need for military leaders to "cherish" the men they lead into battle, the way Hrothgar cherished Aeschere, and wept at his death, is an expression of *comitatus*. The Marines at the Chosin Reservoir demonstrated that the stronger the bonds of *comitatus* among war-fighters, the more likely they are to survive and win in battle. The Army at the Chosin Reservoir demonstrated that the weaker the bonds of *comitatus* among war-fighters, the more likely they are to be defeated and killed in battle.

U.S. military training sank to a nadir in the Vietnam War. Men were drafted from various parts of the country into the military for a one-year-tour in Vietnam. Many times, the commanding officer only spent about 6 months as the leader of his unit. [cxlii] This did not foster strong unit cohesiveness and resilience. The result "was to produce an army of anomic individuals, with no stake in victory and no goal but survival." [cxliii] Perhaps, if American leaders had learned the lesson of the importance of *comitatus* from *Beowulf,* the outcome in Vietnam might have been different.

The concept of *comitatus* does not apply simply to the war-fighters in the field. There must also be a bond of support between the combatants in the field and the society that sent them to war; otherwise the war effort becomes unsustainable. The strength of the bond of *comitatus* between the American public and the American war-fighter in Vietnam was a tenuous one at best. As a result, the North Vietnamese transformed a tactical defeat into a strategic victory by irrevocably weakening the bond of *comitatus* between American civilians and war-fighters after the Tet offensive.

In January 1968, the North Vietnamese violated a truce and launched a massive attack on dozens of cities across South Vietnam. After several weeks of hard fighting, U.S. and South Vietnamese forces drove back the enemy forces and reasserted control across the country. The Communists suffered massive losses, with estimates as high as 50,000 of their troops killed. There were about two thousand American and four thousand South Vietnamese forces killed in the Tet offensive. This was a terrible defeat for the North's military, but Americans watching television at home did not know this. All they saw were videos of death and destruction across South Vietnam. On February 27, 1968, the respected news broadcaster Walter Cronkite said on the air that it was "more certain than ever that the bloody experience of Vietnam is to end in a stalemate." As a result, the spirit of *comitatus,* or the bond of trust between the American people, politicians, and the military, was weakened to such a degree that America as a society lost the will to fight and was eventually forced to withdraw from the field of defeat. [cxliv] [cxlv]

The Vietnam War marked a turning point in American culture. Throughout most of America's history the bond of *comitatus* between ordinary Americans, the military, intellectuals, and political leaders had been very strong, and unabashed patriotism, unqualified support of the military, and military service were common. Retired Lt. Colonel Ralph Peters writes:

> One of the few negative developments in American life over the past half-century has been the loss of ideals of service amongst the most privileged An insider's path in our government, punctuated by spells in think tanks or in temporary professorships, is not one of genuine service, but of self-service. One of the few actual—as opposed to mythic—legacies of Vietnam has been the abdication by the most fortunate Americans of their responsibility to serve in uniform; our nation's favored young took their opposition to one war as a license to turn their backs on our military permanently. As a result, those likeliest to rise to high office lack not only a sense of war's complexity and vagaries, but of the human beings inside our country's uniforms… [cxlvi]

Kathy Roth-Douquet and Frank Schaeffer write in their book *AWOL: the Unexcused Absence of America's Upper Classes from Military Service and How it Hurts Our Country* that the view of military service as "something to be prized and encouraged by all classes" ᶜˣˡᵛⁱⁱ was common in American society until the 1960's. For example, 400 of 750 in Princeton's graduating class in 1956 went into the military. In contrast, nine of Princeton's graduating class in 2004 entered the services, and it had the highest number of graduates going into the military of any Ivy League school in that year. Roth-Douquet and Schaeffer speculate that "an anti-military college culture that may once have had political roots in the Vietnam era has now deteriorated into plain elitism and a set of fossilized, unchallenged antimilitary assumptions." ᶜˣˡᵛⁱⁱⁱ This breakdown of *comitatus* in American culture, between the Americans who serve in the military and the elites who benefit the most in American society, is a strategic weakness exposed by the Communists in the Vietnam War. Enemies will undoubtedly try to exploit it in the future.

Comitatus is a linchpin of modern counterinsurgency warfare. The strategic center of gravity that must be won in unconventional, low-intensity conflicts is the support of the civilian population, the hearts and minds of the people who live where the conflict is taking place. If the war-fighters can create a bond with the local population and convince them that they are there to help, that they are willing to fight and die for them, and if the local population reciprocates, then the combination of skilled war-fighters bound together by *comitatus* with a supportive population is one that is virtually unbeatable.

The strategy of the American military in the Vietnam War under General William Westmorland was to kill or capture as many of the enemy forces as possible. It relied heavily on suspect body counts of enemy dead as a metric of its effectiveness. This strategy placed a low priority on protecting the civilian population of South Vietnam. In fact, it created a perverse incentive for American warfighters to kill as many Vietnamese as possible, regardless of their political allegiances. It did not create a bond of *comitatus* with the Vietnamese people or convince them that the U.S. military was a force for good in their lives. There were, however, rare exceptions, times and place in Vietnam where U.S. troops did not pursue a strategy of attrition but rather tried to protect the population from the North Vietnamese Communist attack. Bing West, in his classic work *The Village,* tells the story of a "Combined Action Platoon" (CAP) that was able to establish the bond of *comitatus* with the people in the Vietnamese village of Binh Nghia by living in Fort Page, a small, fortified position, within the village, patrolling the area around it night and day, and never leaving the villagers to face the enemy alone. The CAP platoon, made up of U.S. Marines and South Vietnamese soldiers, held the village in spite of repeated attacks by numerically superior forces of Viet Cong and North Vietnamese forces.

The CAP became such a thorn in the side of the North Vietnamese that they decided to attack the Marines and their Vietnamese comrades with overwhelming force and crush them. The American forces, which consisted of only 12 Marines, knew they were about to be attacked by around 300 North Vietnamese. The Marines were given the opportunity to withdraw to the safety of a large U.S. military base. The villagers also knew of the impending assault and that the Marines had the option to pull out of the village. Everyone knew the vengeful communists would punish or kill anyone they thought had in any way collaborated with or supported the Americans. The senior Maine non-commissioned Officer of the CAP gave his Marines the chance to vote on either staying to fight against overwhelming odds and facing almost certain death, or abandoning the village and surviving, but leaving the Vietnamese to a horrific fate at the hands of Communists. West records the response of one of the Marines:

> You can go to hell..." he shouted. "You can all go to hell... Screw your vote. I don't give a crap what any of you do... I'm not going to run from those little bastards. I'm going to stay here and blast them. They're not getting this fort. They're not getting this fort. They're not getting this ville. I'm not leaving here no matter what. And you are not getting me out of here..." For several seconds no one spoke... Then [another marine] said... "It was all for nothing if we leave now..." "Yeh," [another marine] said. "There's no way I can see bugging out now." cxlix

The Marines did not abandon the villagers. They resolved to say and fight, even though they had every reason to believe they would be completely overrun and killed or worse by the enemy. The Marines' passionate refusal to leave the South Vietnamese villagers at their time of greatest need echoes Wiglaf's revulsion at the thought of abandoning Beowulf to certain death.

That night, after the meeting was over and the Marines had positioned themselves in preparation for the enemy onslaught, the village was infiltrated by enemy scouts. When one of the village defenders shot one of them, the other scouts "scurried" away, presumably with the information that the village was well-defended. The North Vietnamese did not attack. West concludes:

> In a sense, it was the most important battle the Americans at Fort Page ever prepared to fight. They had chosen to stay; the PF's [Popular Forces militia, which were armed villagers] knew it, and soon so would the entire village. [cl]

The Marines had demonstrated their loyalty to the people of the village, even if it could have resulted in their death. This modern-day manifestation of *comitatus* acted as a force multiplier that allowed them to defend the village against superior forces. Vietnam War veteran USMC Lt. General Gene Duncan wrote, "the combined action program was the most successful thing going in Viet Nam in accomplishing our strategic purpose of winning the minds of the people and in putting the communists out of business." [cli]

Comitatus is as important for war-fighters now as it was for the tenth-century Anglo-Saxons when they wrote down *Beowulf.* What is new about contemporary warfare is that it is not just a bond between war-fighters, nor is it just a bond between war-fighters and the society that supports them; it is also a bond between war-fighters and the civilian population caught in the midst of an armed conflict. Perhaps if Americans had studied *Beowulf* more closely, they would have understood the significance of *comitatus,* created more CAPs in Vietnam, and the war in Vietnam would have turned out differently.

The counterinsurgency strategy put into place in Iraq by General Petreus in 2007 emphasizes defense against harm of the Iraqi population and the development of a civil society that improves their quality of life. As part of this strategy, U.S. war-fighters have been taken out of large, fixed bases and imbedded into Iraqi units to live, fight, and if necessary die side by side with the Iraqis, creating the bond of *comitatus* between American war-fighters, Iraqi war-fighters, and the Iraqi people. There has also been a concerted effort to help rebuild civil society in Iraq. This helps create a bond of *comitatus* not just with the Iraqis, but also with the American public, which is supportive of efforts promoting the construction of roads, schools, and other infrastructure, as well as the development of free markets, rule of law, and some form of liberal democracy. The stronger this bond becomes, the weaker Al-Qaeda in Iraq will become, and if the bond holds Al-Qaeda will almost certainly be defeated.

The *Wall Street Journal* published an editorial entitled "General McChrystal's New Way of War" on 17 June 2009, which discusses how the commander in Afghanistan, General McChrystal, has created a corps of about 400 officers whose careers will focus on Afghanistan. They will deploy to Afghanistan, and when they leave the Afghan theater of operations and return home, they will continue to study issues confronting American and allied war-fighters in theater. They will then redeploy to

Afghanistan, creating a cadre of officers with expertise in Afghan affairs as well as personal connections with Afghan nationals, because in "tribal society like Afghanistan's, the key to effectiveness is having personal relationships with tribal elders." [clii] the "new way of war" is to create the ancient bond of *comitatus* between the war-fighter and the population.

Is *comitatus* always a good thing? The modern age has seen groups of people, such as those who served in the *Wehrmacht* of Nazi Germany or the Imperial Japanese Army, wholeheartedly embrace the concept of *comitatus*. They were "true comrades… each ready to give up his life for the other, without reflection and without thought of personal loss." [cliii] They were superb soldiers. The consequences were disastrous for everyone. The danger of *comitatus* is that there is a sort of "suppression of self-awareness to comradeship" [cliv] and a potential willingness to surrender one's personal honor and moral responsibility to the demands of the group or the leader of the group. The tension in a war-fighter between the values of honor and *comitatus* is never perfectly resolved by any character in Beowulf. Contemporary war-fighters must still try to reconcile the values of honor and*comitatus*. But, can these intangible concepts described in literature be identified, measured, and quantified in real life? In other words, are there any concrete metrics that indicate if a war-fighter is acting with honor, or adhering to the code of comitatus?

There are. These are discussed in the next chapter.

CHAPTER 8
Berserkers: Murder, Mutiny, and Mayhem When Honor and Comitatus Fail

Honor and a sense of *comitatus* are fundamental for any real flesh-and-blood fighting force to be effective. When they are missing in a war fighter, the result is a disaster, exemplified by the berserker. In Old Norse, the term literally means "bear shirt." According to the *Heimskringla,* or the Chronicle of the Kings of Norway, written by Snorri Sturlson around 1225 AD, berserkers belong to the god Odin, the Valfather, or the god of the slain. They were "mad as dogs or wolves, bit their shields, and were as strong as bears or wild bulls, and killed people at a blow, but neither fire nor iron told upon themselves." [clv] They were war-fighters who could somehow shed part of their humanity and become a sort of wild animal in human form.

They would work themselves into the berserker state before battle, possibly with the aid of drugs, and would start behaving like wild animals, howling and biting, then rush into battle without any armor and slaughter their terrified enemies. The berserkers were closely related in the Norse mind to the concept of a shape-shifter, or someone who could take on animal form. *Egil's Saga,* which was first written down around the thirteenth century, contains a description of one man alleged to be a shape-shifter, Kveldulf, which literally means "evening wolf:"

> Every day towards evening he would grow so bad-tempered that few people dared even address him. He always went to sleep early in the evening and woke up early in the morning. People claimed he was a shape-shifter... It is said that people who could take on the character of animals, or went berserk, became so strong in this state that no one was a match for them. clvi

Berserkers are paradoxical figures in Scandinavian literature. On the one hand, they are admired but also feared as ferocious fighters gifted with supernatural powers and valuable in battle. On the other hand, off the battlefield they are typically portrayed as misfits who are none too bright, perhaps a bit emotionally unstable, and a menace to society when not directed at the enemy in a battle. If and when they are killed in a saga, there is "usually very little regret, and a great deal of relief among the locals." clvii We don't know exactly what the berserkers were, but they were considered dangerous enough for the Scandinavians eventually to punish anyone who went into the berserk state. clviii

Descriptions of berserk behavior can also be found in the literature of other cultures. In *The Iliad*, Achilles goes berserk after the death of his comrade Patrocles. He tells Hector that he has shed his humanity and become like a wild beast: "I'll have no talk of pacts with you, as between men and lions there are none, no concord between wolves and sheep, but all hold one another hateful through and through so there can be no courtesy." clix

Achilles proceeds to go on a rampage on the battlefield. He:

crushed dead men and shields. His axle tree [of his chariot] was splashed with blood, so was his chariot rail, with drops thrown up by wheels and horses hooves, and Peleus son [Achilles] kept riding for his glory, staining his powerful arms with mere [feces from the terrified Trojans] and blood. [clx]

The state of beast-like rage and ferocity combined with godlike strength Achilles experienced in Homer's epic is very similar to the berserker state described in Norse literature. In this state, there is a loss of any sense of honor or *comitatus* or even awareness of the world around the berserkers as they attack their enemies.

Ancient literature once again predicts modern life. Ernst Junger was a front-line German soldier in World War I. In his classic work, *Storm of Steel,* he describes what one attack was like for him:

The great moment was at hand. The wave of fire had trundled up to the first lines. We attacked. Our rage broke like a storm. Thousands must have fallen already. That was clear; and even though the shelling continued, it felt quiet... No man's land was packed tight with attackers, advancing singly, in little groups or great masses towards the curtain of fire. They didn't run or even take cover if the vast plume of an explosion rose between them. Ponderous, but unstoppable, they advanced on the enemy lines. It was as though nothing could hurt them anymore... In my right hand, I gripped my pistol, in my left a bamboo riding-crop... As we advanced... The overwhelming desire to kill lent wings to my stride. Rage squeezed bitter tears from my eyes. The immense desire to destroy that overhung the battlefield precipitated a red mist in our brains. We called out sobbing and stammering fragments of sentences to one another, and an impartial observer might have concluded that we were all ecstatically happy. [clxi]

On that day, Ernst Junger was one of Odin's men. It is not just World War I veterans who describe having had berserker experiences. One Vietnam veteran said of his tour in combat:

I lost all mercy... I just couldn't get enough. I built up such hate; I couldn't' do enough damage... Got worse as time went by. I really loved fucking killing, couldn't get enough. For every one that I killed, I felt better. Made some of the hurt go away... I got very hard, cold, merciless, I lost all mercy... [clxii]

When soldiers are facing certain death, the berserk state has a survival value, because they have nothing to lose and everything to gain from reckless frenzy. The incredible strength of individuals in the berserk state, described in the Norse Sagas and by Homer, may be based on real-life situations where war-fighters, either through drugs or through chemicals occurring naturally in their body, such as adrenaline and endogenous endorphins, can transiently improve human performance and block the perception of pain. In this state individuals are not aware of the danger to themselves or their comrades when they attack. They have no restraint on their destructive impulses. They have lost any sense of *comitatus* or honor. One veteran who used to go berserk in Vietnam was eventually "tied up by his own men and taken to the rear while berserk." He has no clear memory of these events, but suspects that he had become a serious threat to them. [clxiii]

The berserk state is a dramatic example of what happens when honor and *comitatus* break down in a warfighter and are replaced with an almost ecstatic delight in death and destruction. Berserkers may kill a lot of the enemy, but they also commit atrocities. As a result, they weaken the essential bond of comitatus between the American war-fighter and the local population where the conflict is taking place, as well as the bond between the American war-fighter and American society as a whole. This is a strategy for disaster and defeat in the low-intensity conflicts of the modern age.

Berserkers do not just injure those around them. They run a great risk of themselves ultimately being consumed and destroyed by the passion of the berserk state. The berserker state:

> is ruinous, leading to the soldiers maiming or death in battle—which is the most frequent outcome—and to lifelong psychological and physical injury if he survives... once a person has entered the berserk state he or she is changed forever... If a soldier survives the berserk state, it imparts emotional deadness and vulnerability to explosive rage to his psychological and a permanent hyper arousal to his physiology—hallmarks of post-traumatic stress disorder in combat veterans. [clxiv]

The war fighter who goes berserk is a menace to friend and foe alike, likely to die to a tragic death in battle or live a life of isolation and loneliness on the margins of society when there are no more battles or wars to be fought.

It is not only individual war-fighters who can succumb to the allure and dangers of the berserk state. In ancient and medieval times it was common for groups of war-fighters to go on rampages of looting, raping, and killing. It can still happen in the modern age. It did happen at My Lai, Vietnam. A U.S. Army platoon led by Second Lieutenant William Calley, Jr., entered the South Vietnamese village of My Lai on March 16, 1968, as part of mission to seek out and destroy Viet Cong. When the soldiers arrived, they found mostly women, children, and old men. If there had been any Viet Cong in the village they had left by the time Calley and his men got there. The details of what happened next are unclear, but the end result was that about 400 unarmed civilians were beaten, stabbed, raped, and ultimately murdered by Calley and his frustrated troops.[clxv] The berserk state in war-fighters is not something that just happened in old stories; it is still with us.

There are other manifestations of a breakdown of honor and *comitatus* in war-fighters besides the berserk state. One is when the war-fighters refuse to go into battle. There was an epidemic of draft-dodging during the Vietnam War, and there were hundreds of "combat refusals" every year in Vietnam where a unit would refuse to fight. Another is when war-fighters murder their leaders to avoid fighting. There were between 800 and 1,000 actual or suspected attempts by American soldiers in Vietnam to murder an officer or NCO through "fragging" or assaults with an explosive weapon. This does not include shootings or misdirected artillery fire aimed at military leaders. Substance abuse is another way to escape the horrors of combat. There was a very high incidence of drug use in the American military in Vietnam.

Atrocities such as the tragedy at My Lai, as well as the number of mutinies, fraggings, and other illegal acts committed by combatants, can be measured and used to as metrics to quantify, at least indirectly, the strength of the code of honor and *comitatus* in war-fighters. Other potential metrics that could indicate when a war-fighter or group of war-fighters is vulnerable to a breakdown in honor and *comitatus* would include the number of PTSD and other mental health-related diagnoses in a unit, the number of drug and alcohol-related incidents, the number of divorces in military families, the reenlistment rate among enlisted personnel, and the retention rate among officers, to name but a few. This information could be used to modify training to foster *comitatus*, or to influence the selection process for leadership positions in order to promote an ethos of honor among war-fighters. For example, Calley's training in Officer Candidate School was accelerated because his unit was due to deploy to Vietnam earlier than expected. [clxvi] It may be that as a result there were shortcuts taken that contributed to Calley and his men losing all restraint at My Lai. Perhaps in the future, such tragedies on the battlefield will be prevented through better training and more attention to signs and risk factors that warn of a breakdown of honor and *comitatus* in war-fighters before it happens.

In the meantime, Americans can do more right now than just measure potential risk factors in war-fighters.

Just as Hrothgar gave gifts to his father's thanes and Hygalec gave Beowulf not just honors but also land and cattle, Americans can provide tangible support for war-fighters. Service members currently receive medical care if they are injured, but there are limited resources. They should be expanded to meet the new generation of warriors returning home injured from Iraq and Afghanistan. Efforts should also be made to improve the medical and social support available to their families. There should be ongoing efforts to ensure that service members have access to educational and employment opportunities during and after their military careers. If we do not take care of our war-fighters, they run the risk of isolation, alienation, and the associated pathologies of substance abuse, PTSD, and other maladies associated with the tragedy of war. The conflicts of the modern age will cost Americans even more dearly in blood and treasure if we do not learn from *Beowulf* the critical importance of cultivating honor and *comitatus* in our war-fighters and in our society as a whole.

CHAPTER 9
Wiglaf's World: The After-Action Report

Beowulf knows he has won great honor by killing the dragon. He also knows he is dying. Wiglaf and the rest of his people will no longer have him to defend them in a hard, brutal world. He does not despair. Instead, he gives thanks to God for his victory. His seeks to follow the code of honor and *comitatus* even after death; he asks Wiglaf to have his ashes interred under a barrow along the cliffs to commemorate his victory and act as a landmark to help guide seafarers through treacherous waters.

After the death of Beowulf there are no more terrible monsters, nor are there any larger-than-life heroes. It is the end of the mythical, heroic age and the beginning of historical times, when tribes and nations like the Swedes and Geats fight against one another in a struggle for power. The world is a bleak place, and the future looks grim. But, it is not a world without hope. There are those like Wiglaf who adhere to the code of honor and of *comitatus*, even at the risk of their own lives, in order to defend their people. This was the reality of life for the Anglo-Saxon audience who heard this poem in the tenth century, and it is still true today.

When Beowulf defends Heorot hall and the people who eat, drink, sing songs, and tell stories there, he is defending civilization. The contrast between the physical, emotional, and spiritual comforts the Danes enjoy during the celebrations held at Heorot and the misery of Grendel and his mother in their cave beneath a lake dramatizes the virtues and benefits of life in an orderly, prosperous civil society. There are those today who would argue that there is no way to judge the superiority of one culture or society over another, and that, therefore, there is no country or culture that is worth fighting and dying for. This is not just nihilistic, it is absurd. Try going without books or television, or hot water or electricity, or modern dentistry for a while. Spend a night sleeping in a banquet hall one night and a cave the next. Think about a child with meningitis who cannot get antibiotics. Civil society is worth defending.

To create and defend such a society requires strength and courage, embodied by Shield Sheafson and his descendants. In times of dire need, its defense may also require unconventional war-fighting skills like those possessed by Beowulf. These military capabilities are only effective if the society appreciates the tragic inevitability of death and destruction in war. Those Enlightenment-minded thinkers who have abandoned this tragic vision and replaced it with a utopian faith in the perfectibility of man do not appreciate the frailty of civilization and the need constantly to defend it. War is incomprehensible to them, and they are often unwilling and always unprepared to defend themselves.

Sun Tzu, in the *Art of War,* written centuries ago, opens his book with the statement that warfare "is the greatest affair of state, the basis of life and death, the Way (Tao) to survival or extinction. It must be thoroughly pondered and analyzed." [clxvii] Several thousand years later, the modern Israeli academic Martin Van Creveld makes a similar observation on the importance of studying warfare: "History is full of the corpses of those who would not or could not defend themselves." [clxviii] *Beowulf* is a distillation of the Anglo-Saxon experience of warfare and conflict. In tribal societies like the one portrayed in *Beowulf,* the study and analysis of conflict was done through edifying myths, legends, and stories, like *Beowulf.* As time passed, story and myth were slowly transformed into history. From the duel between the shepherd boy David and the Philistine giant Goliath, to the battle of Thermopylae, where a few hundred Spartans and allied troops sacrificed their lives to hold off a massive Persian army long enough to allow the Greeks to organize themselves and ultimately defeat the invading force, to the Battle of Malta in 1565, where some 700-odd knights and 8,000 auxiliary forces defeated a 40,000-man force sent by the Ottoman Sultan Sulamein the Magnificent to destroy them, history is filled with lessons on the value of honor and *comitatus* to war-fighters of many cultures and civilizations.

In our own time, in the second battle of Fallujah in 2004, the U.S. military decided to minimize the use of aerial bombing and artillery shelling in an effort to limit the counterproductive, tragic loss of civilian life in the city. Instead, there were dozens and dozens of "knife fights in a phone booth" as American and Coalition war-fighters went from house to house, relying on small arms, clenched fists, a strong grip, and the occasional arm lock to defeat Al-Qaeda and other terrorists hiding in the dark, empty, cavernous, buildings of the city. Literature and history teaches us that battles are decided not just by the numbers of combatants and their equipment and armaments, but also by the spirit of honor and *comitatus* of the war-fighters, if are just willing to learn.

Unfortunately, Americans seem unwilling to follow the advice of Sun Tzu or Van Creveld and study warfare. Most of the things written about *Beowulf* nowadays explore issues like the Christian and Pagan components of the poem, the structure of Anglo-Saxon poetry, gender roles in the poem, and many other topics that are of great interest to academics but would have been of secondary interest to the Anglo-Saxons struggling for survival in the tenth century. The possibility of learning something from the poem applicable to modern warfare receives little if any attention in the modern age.

The reason for this is somewhat unclear. It may be a result of a revulsion felt toward war in the Western world after the First or Second World Wars, or a result of changes in academia on college campuses across America after the Vietnam War. Or perhaps the fact that very few professors have served in the military. For whatever reasons, Americans neglect the study of military history in general. Out of several thousand U.S. universities, each of which teaches dozens and dozens of courses, only a handful of them offer any courses in military history. [clxix] As a result, Americans are less prepared than they could be to understand and respond to the armed conflicts that continue to break out all the time, all over the world. The integration of the study of literature and history from the perspective of a war-fighter into a liberal arts education, perhaps with an occasional combat veteran invited to lecture at the university or college campus, would be the first steps toward creating an American people who understand the tragic nature of violent conflicts as well as the critical importance of honor and *comitatus* for war-fighters to be victorious in combat. In the meantime, until these changes are put into place, read *Beowulf*.

ENDNOTES

[i] Seamus Heaney, Beowulf: A New Verse Translation (New York: W.W. Norton and Company, 2000).

[ii] Ibid, pp. 3-5

[iii] Ibid.

[iv] Ibid, p. 7

[v] Ibid, p. 23

[vi] Ibid, p. 7

[vii] Ibid, p. 95

[viii] Ibid, p. 13

[ix] Ibid, p. 15

[x] Ibid, pp. 15-17

[xi] Ibid, p. 39

[xii] Ibid, p. 41

[xiii] Ibid, p. 33

[xiv] Ibid, p. 47

[xv] Ibid. p. 51

xvi Ibid, p. 53

xvii Ibid, p. 55

xviii Ibid.

xix Ibid, p. 87

xx Ibid, p. 89

xxi Ibid, p. 97

xxii Ibid, pp. 95-101

xxiii Ibid, p. 101

xxiv Ibid, pp. 103-115

xxv Ibid, p. 121

xxvi Ibid, p. 157

xxvii Ibid.

xxviii Ibid, p. 159

xxix Ibid p. 163

xxx Ibid, p. 171

xxxi Ibid, p. 173

xxxii Ibid.

xxxiii Ibid, p. 179

xxxiv Ibid, p. 181

xxxv Ibid, p. 189

xxxvi Ibid, p. 193

xxxvii Ibid.

xxxviii Ibid, pp. 197-203

xxxix Ibid, p. 207

xl Ibid, p. 213

xli Ibid, p. 3

xlii Ibid, p. 7

xliii Ibid, p. 31

xliv Ibid, p. 7

xlv Ibid, p. 95

xlvi Ibid, p. 33

xlvii Ibid, p. 13

xlviii Robert B. Asprey, War in the Shadows (Lincoln, NE: Universe, Inc, 2002), pp. 3-35

xlix Martin Van Creveld, The Transformation of War (New York, NY: Simon and Schuster, 1991), pp. 1-35

l Stanley Karnow, Vietnam: A History (New York, NY: Penguin, 1997) p. 450

li Ernest Evans, Wars Without Splendor: The U.S. Military and Low-Level Conflict (New York, NY: Greenwood Press, 1987), pp. 132-36 lii Michael Yon, Moment of Truth in Iraq (USA: Richard Vigilante Books, 2008), pp. 6-13

liii Seamus Heaney, Beowulf: A New Verse Translation (New York: W. W. Norton and Company, 2000), p. 9

liv Life Application Study Bible (Grand Rapids, MI: Tyndale House Publishers, 1997), pp. 4-5

lv Leon Kass, The Beginning of Wisdom (Chicago, Il: The University of Chicago Press, 2003), pp. 144-46

lvi Seamus Heaney, Beowulf: A New Verse Translation (New York: W. W. Norton and Company, 2000), p. 105

lvii Ibid, p. 95

lviii David Galula, Counterinsurgency Warfare: Theory and Practice (Westport, CT: Praeger Security International), p. 24

lix Seamus Heaney, Beowulf: A New Verse Translation (New York: W. W. Norton and Company, 2000), p. 89

lx Ibid, p. 91

lxi Ibid, p. 9

lxii Ibid, p. 13

lxiii Ibid, pp. 13-15

lxiv Michael Yon, Moment of Truth in Iraq (United States: Richard Vigilante), p. 11

lxv Ibid, p. 12

lxvi Seamus Heaney Beowulf: A New Verse Translation (New York: W. W. Norton and Company, 2000), p. 19

lxvii Ibid, p. 149

lxviii Ibid.

lxix Ibid, p. 19

lxx Ibid, p. 25

lxxi Ibid, p. 27

lxxii Ibid.

lxxiii Ibid, p. 29

lxxiv Ibid. p. 3

lxxv Ibid, p. 5

lxxvi Ibid, p. 49

lxxvii Ibid, p. 53

lxxviii Ibid, p. 111

lxxix Ibid, p. 11

lxxx Ibid, p. 9

lxxxi Ibid, p. 7

lxxxii Ibid, p. 211

lxxxiii Peter Foote, David M. Wilson, The Viking Achievement (London, England: Book Club Associates, 1973), pp. 390-91

lxxxiv James Earl, Thinking about Beowulf (Stanford, CA: Stanford University Press, 1994), p. 53

lxxxv Ibid, p. 51

lxxxvi Jonathan Shay, Achilles in Vietnam: Combat Trauma and the Undoing of Character (New York, NY, 1994), pp. 146-48

lxxxvii Ibid, pp. 155-56

lxxxviii Life Application Study Bible(Grand Rapids, MI: Tyndale House Publishers, 1997. Genesis 3:17-19

lxxxix Ibid, Job 7:105, 7-20

xc Robert Brown Mcfee, Ed., The Essential Reinhold Niebuhr (New Haven, CT: Yale University Press, 1986), p. 125

xci Robert D. Kaplan, Warrior Politics (Random House: NY, 2003), pp. xxi, 80-81

xcii Ibid, p. 88

xciii Reinhold Nieburh, The Nature and Destiny of Man (Louisville, KY: 1996), p. 23

xciv Peggy Noonan, "Remembering the Dawn of the Age of Abundance," http://online.wsj.com/article/SB123508142847026881.html

[xcv] Georges Sada, Saddam's Secrets (Brentwood, TN: Integrity Publishers, 2006), p. 7

[xcvi] Victor Davis Hanson, "A Long War in a Nutshell: A Look Back," (2007) http://victorhanson.com/articles/hanson122907.html

[xcvii] Seamus Heaney, Beowulf: A New Verse Translation (New York: W. W. Norton and Company, 2000), p. 43

[xcviii] Ibid, p. 47

[xcix] Ibid, p. 55

[c] Anthony Everitt, Cicero: the Life and Times of Rome's Greatest Politician (New York, NY: Random House, 2001), p. 46

[ci] Jonathan Shay, Achilles in Vietnam: Combat Trauma and the Undoing of Character (New York, NY: Touchstone, 1994), pp. 58, 67

[cii] Ibid, p. 79

[ciii] Martin Creveld, The Culture of War (New York, NY: Random House, 2008), p. 15

[civ] J. Glenn Grey, The Warriors: Reflections on Men in Battle (Lincoln, NE: University of Nebraska Press, 1970), p. 142

[cv] Omer Bartov, Hitler's Army (New York, NY: Oxford University Press, 1992), pp. 130-31

[cvi] Ibid, p. 184

cvii Grey, p. 144

cviii John Dower, War Without Mercy (New York, NY: Pantheon Books, 1986), pp. 215-17

cix Ibid, pp. 7-10, 215-17

cx Grey, p. 152

cxi Ibid, p. 180

cxii Shay, p. 106

cxiii Ibid.

cxiv Ibid, p. 116

cxv Ibid, p. 119

cxvi Ibid, p. 106

cxvii Bing West, The Strongest Tribe (New York: Random House, 2008), p. 9.

cxviii Ibid, p. 12

cxix Ibid, p. 247

cxx Ibid, p. 109

cxxi Ibid, p. 123

cxxii H. R. McMaster, Dereliction of Duty, (New York, NY: Harper Collins Publishers, 1997) pp. 33-34

cxxiii Ibid, p. 19

cxxiv Ibid, p. 21

cxxv Ibid, p. 327

cxxvi Ibid, p. 330

cxxvii Ibid, p. 334

cxxviii Cornelius Tacitus, The Agricoloa and the Germania (Stillwell, KS: Digireads.com Publishing, 2008), p. 51

cxxix John Grigsby, Beowulf and Grendel (London: Watkins Publishing, 2005), p. 23

cxxx Seamus Heaney, Beowulf: A New Verse Translation (New York: W. W. Norton and Company, 2000), pp. 21, 33

cxxxi Ibid, p. 27

cxxxii Ibid, p. 111

cxxxiii Ibid, p. 156, 169

cxxxiv Dave Grossman and Loren Christensen, On Combat (China: Warrior Science Publications, 2008) p. 9

cxxxv Robert Cook, Njal's Saga (London, England: Penguin, 1997), pp. 76-77, 159-60, 170-71

cxxxvi Jonathan Shay, Odysseus in America (New York, NY: Scribner, 2002), p. 208

cxxxvii Martin Van Creveld, The Culture of War (New York, NY: Ballantine Books, 2008), pp. 53-54

cxxxviii Ibid, p. 119

cxxxix Victor Davis Hanson, A War Like No Other (New York, NY: Random House, 2005), p. 134

cxl Christopher Bassford, The Spit-Shine Syndrome (Westport, CN: Greenwood Press, 1988), p. 26

cxli Thomas Ricks, Making the Corps (New York, NY: Scribner 1997) pp. 190-92

cxlii Ibid, p. 22

cxliii Christopher Bassford, The Spit-Shine Syndrome (Westport, CN: Greenwood Press, 1988), p. 26

cxliv Stanley Karnow, Vietnam: A History (New York, NY: Penguin Books, 1984), pp. 536-581

cxlv Neil Sheehan, A Bright Shining Lie: John Paul Vann and America in Vietnam (New York, NY: Random House, 1988) p. 708

cxlvi Ralph Peters, New Glory: Expanding America's Global Supremacy (New York, NY: Penguin Group, 2005), p. 72

cxlvii Kathy Roth-Douquet and Frank Schaeffer, AWOL: The Unexcused Absence of America's Upper Class From Military Service and How It Hurts Our Country (New York, NY: Harper Collins, 2006), p. 108

cxlviii Ibid, p. 45

cxlix Bing West, The Village (New York, NY: Pocket Books, 2003), pp. 234-235

cl Ibid, p. 236

cli Gene Duncan, Dunk's Almanac (Gene Duncan, 1982), p. 262

clii Max Boot, "General McChrystal's New Way of War," Wall Street Journal, June 17, 2009 A13

cliii Grey, p. 46

cliv Grey, p. 90

clv Snorri Sturlson, Heimskringla, Translated by Samual Laing, (London, England: Forgotten Books), p. 8

clvi Ornolfur Thorson, ed., The Sagas of the Icelanders (New York, NY: Penguin Books, 1997), p. 8, 46

clvii Ibid, p. 742

clviii Eric Christiansen, The Norsemen in the Viking Age (Malden, MA: Blackwell Publishing, 2006), p. 31

clix Shay, p. 83

clx Ibid, p. 85

clxi Ernst Junger, Storm of Steel, translated by Michael Hofmann, (New York, NY: Penguin Books, 2003) pp. 231-32

clxii Shay, pp. 78-79

clxiii Ibid, p. 87

clxiv Ibid, pp. 98-99

clxv Neil Sheehan, A Bright Shining Lie: John Paul Vann and America in Vietnam (New York, NY: Random House, 1988) p. 689

clxvi Doug Linder, "An Introduction to the My Lai Courts-Martial," http://www.law.umkc.edu/faculty/projects/ftrials/mylai/Myl_intro.html

clxvii Sun Tzu, art of War (Boulder, CO: Westview Press, 1994), p. 167

clxviii Martin Van Creveld, The Culture of War (New York, NY: Random House, 2008), p. 170

clxix Ibid, p. 55, 180

BIBLIOGRAPHY

Asprey, R. B. War in the Shadows. Lincoln, NE: Universe, Inc, 2002.

Bartov, O. Hitler's Army. New York, NY: Oxford University Press, 1992.

Bassford, C. The Spit-Shine Syndrome. Westport, CN: Greenwood Press, 1988.

Boot, M. "General McChrystal's New Way of War." Wall Street Journal, June 17, A13.

Christiansen, E. The Norsemen in the Viking Age. Malden, MA: Blackwell Publishing, 2006.

Cook, R. Njal's Saga. London, England: Penguin, 1997.

Dower, J. War Without Mercy. New York, NY: Pantheon Books, 1986.

Earl, James. Thinking About Beowulf. Stanford, CA: Stanford University Press, 1994.

Evans, E. Wars Without Splendor: The U.S. Military and Low-Level Conflict. New York, NY: Greenwood Press, 1987.

Everitt, A. Cicero: The Life and Time of Rome's Greatest Politician. New York, NY: Random House, 2001.

Foote, P. and Wilson, DM. The Viking Achievement. London, England: Book Club Associates, 1973.

Galula, David. Counterinsurgency Warfare: Theory and Practice. Westport, CT: Praeger Security International, 2006.

Gray, J.G. The Warriors: Reflections on Men in Battle. Nebraska: University of Nebraska Press, 1970.

Grisby, John. Beowulf and Grendel. London: Watkins Publishing, 2005.

Grossman, D. and Christensen, L. On combat. China: Warrior Science Publications, 2008.

Hanson, V.D. A War Like No Other. New York, NY: Random House, 2005.

Hanson, V.D. "A Long War in a Nutshell: A Look Back." 2007. http://victorhanson.com/articles/hanson122907.html.

Heaney, S. Beowulf: A New Verse Translation. New York, NY: Farrar, Strauss and Giroux, 2000.

Junger, Ernst. Storm of Steel. New York, NY: Penguin, 2004.

Kaplan, Robert D. Warrior Politics. New York, NY: Random House, 2003.

Karnow, S. Vietnam: A History. New York, NY: Penguin, 1997.

Kass, L. The Beginning of Wisdom. Chicago, IL: The University of Chicago Press, 2003.

Life Application Study Bible. Grand Rapids, MI: Tyndale House Publishers, 1997.

Linder, Doug. "An Introduction to the My Lai Courts-Martial." http://www.law.umkc.edu/faculty/projects/ftrials/mylai/myl_bcalleyhtml.htm.

Mcfee, Robert Brown, ed. The Essential Reinhold Niebuhr. New Haven, CT: Yale University Press, 1986.

McMaster, H.R. Dereliction of Duty. New York, NY: Harper Collins Publishers, 1997.

Noonan, Peggy. "Remembering the Dawn of the Age of Abundance." http://online.wsj.com/article/SB123508142847026881.html

Peters, R. New Glory: Expanding America's Global Supremacy. New York, NY: Penguin Group, 2005.

Ricks, T. Making the Corps. New York, NY: Scribner, 1997.

Roth-Douquet, K. and Schaeffer, K. AWOL: The Unexcused Absence of America's Upper Class from Military Service and How it Hurts our Country. New York, NY: Harper Collins, 2006.

Sada, Georges. Saddam's Secrets. Brentwood, TN: Integrity Publishers, 2006.

Shay, Jonathan. Achilles in Vietnam: Combat Trauma and the Undoing of Character. New York, NY: Touchstone Books, 1994.

Shay, J. Odysseus in America. New York NY: Scribner, 2002.

Sheehan, N. A Bright Shining Lie: John Paul Vann and America in Vietnam. New York, NY: Random House, 1988.

Short, W. Viking Weapons and Combat Techniques. Yardley, PA: Westholme Publishing, LLC, 2009.

Sun Tzu. Art of War. Boulder, CO: Westview Press, 1994.

Sturlson, S. Heimskringla, or, The Chronicle of the Kings of Norway. Charleston, South Carolina: Forgotten Books, 2008.

Tacitus, C. The Agricola and the Germania. Stillwell, KS: Digireads.com Publishing, 2008.

Thorson, O. ed. The Sagas of the Icelanders. New York, NY: Penguin Books, 1997.

Van Creveld, M. The Culture of War. New York, NY: Random House, 2008.

West, B. The Strongest Tribe. New York, NY: Random House, 2008.

West, B. The Village. New York, NY: Pocket Books, 2003.

Yon, M. Moment of Truth in Iraq. USA: Richard Vigilante Books, 2008.

ABOUT THE AUTHOR

T. M. Johnson graduated with honors in history from Haverford College. He went on to attend the University of Minnesota medical school and became a neurologist. He has extensive clinical experience caring for military service members with traumatic brain injury and post-traumatic stress disorder. He is an avid outdoorsman, and whenever possible will relax by spending time on his ranch in Montana.